PRAISE FOR

"This book provides a comprehensive and updated introduction to sequence analysis. I highly recommend it for anyone who wants to learn the topic systematically."

—Tim F. Liao, University of Illinois at Urbana–Champaign

SEQUENCE ANALYSIS

QUANTITATIVE APPLICATIONS IN THE SOCIAL SCIENCES

SERIES: QUANTITATIVE APPLICATIONS IN THE SOCIAL SCIENCES

Series Editor: Barbara Entwisle, Sociology,
The University of North Carolina at Chapel Hill

Editorial Board

SEQUENCE ANALYSIS

Marcel Raab
State Institute for Family
Research at the University of Bamberg

Emanuela Struffolino
University of Milan

Los Angeles | London | New Delhi
Singapore | Washington DC

FOR INFORMATION:

SAGE Publications, Inc.
2455 Teller Road
Thousand Oaks, California 91320
E-mail: order@sagepub.com

SAGE Publications Ltd.
1 Oliver's Yard
55 City Road
London EC1Y 1SP
United Kingdom

SAGE Publications India Pvt. Ltd.
B 1/I 1 Mohan Cooperative Industrial Area
Mathura Road, New Delhi 110 044
India

SAGE Publications Asia-Pacific Pte. Ltd.
18 Cross Street #10-10/11/12
China Square Central
Singapore 048423

Printed in the United States of America

ISBN: 978-1-0718-0188-8

This book is printed on acid-free paper.

Sponsoring Editor: Helen Salmon
Product Associate: Yumna Samie
Production Editor: Astha Jaiswal
Copy Editor: Diane DiMura & TC
Typesetter: Hurix Digital
Cover Designer: Candice Harman
Marketing Manager: Victoria Velasquez

22 23 24 25 26 10 9 8 7 6 5 4 3 2 1

BRIEF CONTENTS

DETAILED CONTENTS

SERIES EDITOR'S INTRODUCTION

Sequences are characteristic of social life. Conversations are sequences of verbal behavior, romantic relationships are sequences of actions and emotional states, careers are sequences of job positions, the family life course is a sequence of partnership and parenthood transitions, and social movements are sequences of political actions. Each of these social sequences is a series of ordered categorical elements that may be predictable and common to many, or turbulent and highly individualized. In *Sequence Analysis*, Professors Raab and Struffolino provide a state-of-the-art introduction to tools for describing and analyzing whole sequences based on categorical data. Sequences are the units of analysis.

Sequence Analysis is for readers who are new to it and for experienced practitioners. For the former, it provides a clear exposition of concepts and terminology (e.g., alphabet, episode); notation (e.g., DSS, SPS); methods of description (e.g., selection of a "representative" sequence); and helpful visualizations (e.g., state distribution plots, relative frequency sequence plots). It covers classical optimal matching techniques and extensions developed in response to critiques of such matching. More experienced readers will appreciate the discussion of cluster analysis, the analysis of sequence data on multiple trajectories, and various approaches for studying sequences in relation to potential covariates in the later chapters.

Examples are key to the pedagogy. Data on family and employment trajectories from the German Family Panel are used to illustrate the application of the methods. A companion website at **https://sa-book.github.io** contains color versions of the figures as well as the data and R script to replicate the examples. Together, the volume and companion website provide a self-contained collection of materials that would serve well as a supplement to a course in sequence analysis methods, or even on the most important application of these methods, the life course, as well as for self-study.

Professors Raab and Struffolino have extensive experience with sequence analysis methods. *Sequence Analysis* is chock-full of their practical guidance. As they explain, results are sensitive to the many decisions made by analysts, so they discuss these decisions in detail, as well as possible rationales and potential consequences. Throughout, they emphasize the importance of assessing the robustness of results of these decisions and illustrate this as they demonstrate the application of the methods. In the concluding chapter, they provide a list of recommendations that readers should consider in conducting their own sequence analysis, with a particular emphasis on exploring the data thoroughly. Whereas many authors summarize tools and methods, Professors Raab and Struffolino summarize guidance, a very helpful capstone to the volume.

In the history of sequence analysis, there have been three waves. The first wave of sequence analysis was in the late 1980s and 1990s. Critiques of these early approaches led to the second wave, characterized by the refinement and extension of the sequence analysis toolkit. The third wave is currently in progress and involves jointly applying sequence analysis with more established statistical methods. This volume covers all three waves. Not only does it provide a comprehensive introduction to commonly used tools, but it also introduces readers to parts of the field and tools still in development. *Sequence Analysis* unites diverse contributions into an up-to-date and comprehensive short course on how to use the sequence analysis toolkit.

—Barbara Entwisle
Series Editor

ACKNOWLEDGMENTS

We consider this book the fortunate outcome of an even more fortunate encounter: We met in 2012 at the WZB Berlin Social Science Center when working with Anette E. Fasang at her research group on "Demography and Inequality." We are grateful to her for sharing her knowledge of and enthusiasm for sequence analysis, as well as for her support along our academic careers. Our gratitude further extends to the Sage QASS editor, Barbara Entwisle, for facilitating this project, organizing the review process, and making excellent suggestions and comments on earlier versions of this manuscript. We want to thank acquisitions editor Helen Salmon for supporting us throughout the publication process. The final version of the book benefited from thoughtful comments and suggestions by several reviewers, and we are indebted to them for their service. Any remaining errors are our responsibility.

Our collaboration for this project strengthened our conviction that academic work benefits greatly from sharing ideas and passion with researchers from different disciplines. Therefore, we want to thank the Sequence Analysis Association community for being an important space where ideas and passion for sequence analysis can flourish. We thank Camilla Borgna, Christian Brzinsky-Fay, Marianna Filandri, Tim F. Liao, Raffaella Piccarreta, Gilbert Ritschard, Carla Rowold, Matthias Studer, and Zachary Van Winkle for the engaging methodological discussions in the past years, and we are hoping for more in the future. We are grateful for the feedback received from the participants of our workshops at various universities and institutions, as well as the doctoral students and student assistants of the group "MyWealth—Accumulation of Personal Wealth in Couples" at the Humboldt-Universität zu Berlin for comments on some chapters of the book. Finally, we thank the pairfam team for permitting us to share a reduced version of their data for learning and teaching purposes on our companion website.

SAGE and the authors are grateful for feedback from the following reviewers during the development of this text:

Stefany Coxe, Florida International University

Jacques Hagenaars, Tilburg University

David Han, University of Texas, San Antonio

Melanie Hinojosa, University of Central Florida

William Jacoby, Michigan State University

Erin Leahey, University of Arizona

Tim Liao, University of Illinois

Helmut Norpoth, Stony Brook University

PREFACE

The writing of this book followed a nonlinear trajectory and went through several turning points, with episodes of rapid progress, stagnation, and even some detours. In a sense, this process resembled the history of sequence analysis in the social sciences: After the seminal theoretical and empirical works in the late 1980s and early 1990s, we had to wait some years before the increasing availability of longitudinal data provided more opportunities to address sequence-oriented questions. During this period, the sequence analysis toolkit was thoroughly revised and extended. The method matured as many of its initial weaknesses and limitations were addressed. Although some long-standing issues have not yet been resolved, the field is advancing rapidly through a steady flow of innovative methodological contributions and the corresponding development of freely available statistical software.

In view of this progress, this book sees the light in a period in which sequence analysis has developed some well-established standards but still lacks a comprehensive book that not only summarizes its foundations and some of the recent advances but also provides instructions and recommendations on how to apply these methods. Until now, materials on sequence analysis that might serve this purpose are scattered across several journal articles, monographs, edited volumes, and software manuals. This makes it difficult for instructors, students, and researchers to identify a single comprehensive resource covering the basics of sequence analysis and providing guidelines on how to perform methodologically sound analyses.

Therefore, we imagined and wrote this book to be an introduction that guides researchers along the entire workflow of sequence analysis, discussing the repercussions of each involved analytical decision. With the exception of a few recent methodological advances briefly introduced in Chapter 7, we illustrate all techniques presented in the book with real-world survey data from the German Family Panel (pairfam). The volume is accompanied by additional online material available at **https://sa-book.github.io** comprising the R code to reproduce the figures and tables we present throughout this book. Taken together, the online material and the book provide an up-to-date overview of state-of-the-art sequence analysis techniques and equip its readers with the theoretical knowledge and practical skills to conduct their own sequence analysis.

ABOUT THE AUTHORS

Marcel Raab is senior researcher at the State Institute for Family Research at the University of Bamberg and deputy managing director of the *Journal of Family Research*. Previously, he worked as a research assistant at the National Educational Panel Study and the Professorship of Demography at the University of Bamberg, as a research fellow in the research group "Demography and Inequality" at the WZB Berlin Social Science Center, and assistant professor for sociology at the University of Mannheim. In 2011, he was a visiting predoctoral fellow at the Center for Research on Inequalities and the Life Course (CIQLE) at Yale University, New Haven, Connecticut. In 2014, he obtained a doctorate in sociology at the University of Bamberg with his dissertation on "Family Effects on Family Formation." Currently, he is a member of the advisory board of the Sequence Analysis Association.

Emanuela Struffolino is assistant professor of economic sociology at the University of Milan, Department of Social and Political Sciences. Between 2020 and 2021, she was guest professor of macrosociology at the Institute of Sociology at the Freie Universität Berlin and then guest professor of social policy at the Humboldt-Universität zu Berlin. From 2015 to 2019, she was a postdoctoral fellow at the research group "Demography and Inequality" research group at the WZB Berlin Social Science Center. After obtaining her PhD in sociology at the University of Milano-Bicocca, in 2014 she worked as a research fellow at the Swiss National Centre for Competence in Research "LIVES—Overcoming Vulnerability: A Life-Course Perspective" at the University of Lausanne. She is a member of the executive board of the Sequence Analysis Association.

Both authors regularly teach courses and workshops on sequence analysis and have conducted several studies using sequence analysis that have been published in *Demography*, *European Journal of Population*, *Research in Social Stratification and Mobility*, *Sociological Methodology*, *Demographic Research*, *Advances in Life Course Research*, and *Social Indicators Research*.

CHAPTER 1

INTRODUCTION

1.1 Sequence Analysis in the Social Sciences

Studying sequences of events or (temporally) ordered social processes is a primary concern of social sciences. In psychology, sociology, and political science, sequences figure prominently in various kinds of stage theories. Similarly, sequences are central to scholars engaged in life course sociology or life span psychology. Moreover, sequences are scrutinized in other fields of human and social sciences such as anthropology, archaeology, geography, and economics (for a more detailed discussion, see Abbott, 1995; Blanchard, 2019; and Cornwell, 2015). Given this broad interest coming from different branches of social sciences, it is not surprising that we encounter a wide variety of definitions and analytical tools in the largely disconnected literature on this topic. As a result, a wide range of quantitative methods as diverse as mixed latent Markov models, event history analysis, and panel regressions have been discussed as tools for analyzing sequence data. All of these methods are representatives of the so-called stochastic modeling culture and thus are based on stochastic assumptions regarding the data-generating process (Aisenbrey & Fasang, 2010; Breiman, 2001; Piccarreta & Studer, 2018). In addition, most of them share the focus on studying single or repeated transitions rather than the process as a whole. These methods are well-established, widely used, and partly also covered in previous volumes of this book series (Allison, 2009, 2014; Preacher et al., 2008).

The present volume is dedicated to a different set of analytical tools, sometimes referred to as *whole sequence methods* for categorical data or simply *sequence analysis* (SA). These tools were first introduced to social sciences in the form of optimal matching (OM) analysis by Andrew Abbott (Abbott & Forrest, 1986; Abbott & Hrycak, 1990), who imported this approach from biology and computer science (Levenshtein, 1966; Sankoff & Kruskal, 1983). OM analysis quantifies the degree of dissimilarity between sequences. In contrast to the methods just mentioned, OM and several of the SA tools have their roots in the data mining or algorithmic modeling culture and thus do not make any assumptions on the data-generating process. Accordingly, SA lends itself particularly well to studying exploratory and descriptive research questions. More specifically, SA tools are usually applied to (a) describe and (b) visualize sequences, (c) identify typical patterns among a set of sequences, and (d) examine the antecedents and consequences of these patterns (Abbott, 1990; Vanhoutte et al., 2018).

SA conceptualizes social sequences as a series of—usually temporally—ordered categorical elements. It has been applied for studying processes as diverse as labor market entry sequences (distinguishing states such as "education," "employed," "unemployed," "inactive"; e.g., Brzinsky-Fay, 2007); partnership biographies (e.g., "single," "living apart together," "cohabiting," "married"; e.g., Raab & Struffolino, 2019); pathways toward democratization ("parliamentary democracy," "presidential democracy," "military dictatorship," "monarchy"; Wilson, 2014); time use of couples ("nobody is working," "both partners are working," "only one partner is working"; Lesnard, 2008); actual and idealized relationship scripts ("meet partner's parents," "go out alone," "hold hands," "kiss," "sexual intercourse"; Soller, 2014); or basic types of figures in ritual dances ("once-to-yourself," "footing," "partners," "rounds," "hey"; Abbott & Forrest, 1986).

SA treats sequences as units of analysis. Instead of studying specific transitions between states or events in isolation, SA puts them into context by simultaneously considering the timing, ordering, and duration of all the states that make up a sequence. It thus acknowledges that the meaning and the consequences of social facts usually can be fully understood only by considering "their larger sequential context" (Cornwell, 2015). The various pathways leading to an identical labor market status at age 45, for instance, can differ considerably, which in turn can have severe consequences for the accumulation of wealth, marital status, or health outcomes.

In the first 10 to 15 years after its introduction to the social sciences, SA was predominantly used for identifying patterns in sequences by means of OM analysis (Abbott & Tsay, 2000; Aisenbrey & Fasang, 2010; MacIndoe & Abbott, 2004). This procedure involves three analytical steps: defining a coding scheme for the elements constituting the sequences (see previous examples for different processes), computing pairwise dissimilarities between sequences, and identifying patterns applying multidimensional scaling or clustering to the dissimilarity matrix obtained in the second step. The resulting clusters are used as either an independent or a dependent variable in a regression analysis to examine the determinants or consequences of specific sequence patterns. This standard procedure of analytical steps still prevails in SA today, although the methodological tools have been continuously refined and expanded since then. Most of these advances were developed in the aftermath of the "2000 controversy" (Aisenbrey, 2017) in the journal *Sociological Methods & Research,* in which SA's algorithmic modeling culture and the data handling of optimal matching analysis have been heavily criticized (Levine, 2000; Wu, 2000). Ten years later, the same journal published a special issue on SA in which Aisenbrey and Fasang (2010) provided an excellent overview of the initial critique of classical optimal matching applications and the following methodological advancements aptly referred to as the "second wave of sequence analysis," which mainly extended OM and introduced other techniques to compare sequences. In the present volume, we will introduce both the classical optimal matching approach as well as analytical tools of the so-called second wave. In addition, we briefly highlight some more recent advances we consider to be the third wave of SA. This wave is largely characterized by the effort of bringing together the stochastic and the algorithmic modeling cultures by jointly applying SA with more established methods such as analysis of variance, event history, network analysis, or causal analysis in general (Barban et al., 2017; Cornwell, 2015; Piccarreta & Studer, 2018; Ritschard & Studer, 2018; Studer et al., 2011).

In sum, the field of SA is undergoing a burgeoning development since the early contributions in the 1980s that is clearly favored by the increasing availability of suitable (longitudinal) data and software packages. Particularly since the 2000s and within the disciplines of sociology and demography, this development is accompanied by an increasing number of publications in renowned journals that contribute to the overall visibility of the method beyond the small but steadily growing community of SA experts.

It is beyond the scope of this book to provide a comprehensive review of all the new and diverse SA tools that have been developed in recent years, nor do we strive for giving a full account of the history of sequence analysis in the social sciences. Instead, this book aims to equip researchers with the knowledge necessary to conduct their own SA. We introduce the basic concepts and techniques of SA but also consider many of the more recent developments, which to date have only been described scattered across several journal articles, book chapters, and software documentation. The book discusses the implication of the typical analytical choices involved in conducting a sequence analysis and provides several guidelines and recommendations. By covering the foundations as well as up-to-date summaries of current discussions on the key analytical steps of SA in one resource, this book addresses both readers who are new to the method and those who already used it in their research. The following section provides an overview clarifying which chapters might be of interest to these different groups of readers.

1.2 Organization of the Book

Figure 1.1 displays the structure and content of the following chapters. In Chapter 2, we first introduce the basic concepts and terminology of SA

Figure 1.1 The workflow of sequence analysis

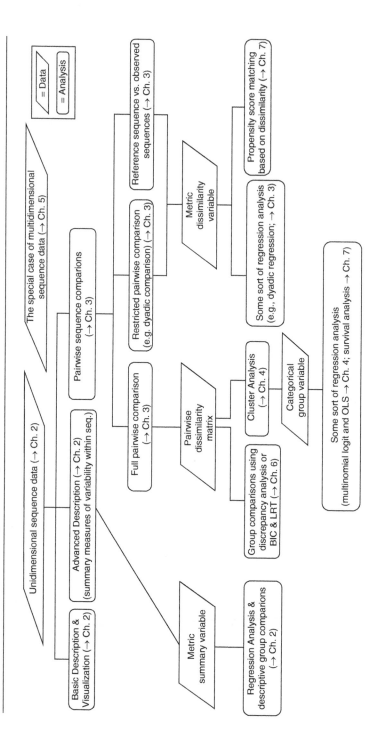

before we proceed to the critical task of defining meaningful sequences and touch upon the issue of handling missing data. Once these conceptual foundations are laid, we introduce tools to explore sequences by tabulating their properties and visualizing them with insightful graphs. Descriptive exploration includes simple counts of sequence frequencies, time spent in different states, transition rates between different states, and state patterns. Although these descriptive analyses provide a useful first overview, they might be somewhat overwhelming because they summarize the sequence data by presenting a lot of different numbers. Therefore, we introduce more advanced descriptors that either just summarize the diversity of individual sequences by calculating composite indices such as sequence complexity and turbulence, or try to assess the quality of status changes within sequences by discriminating between positive and negative transitions (e.g., from unemployment to employment or vice versa). Conveying much information in a single indicator, these composite indices are interesting by themselves, but we will also show that they are well-suited for being used as dependent or independent variables in regression analyses.

Chapter 3 is dedicated to the "core business" (Gauthier et al., 2014) and arguably also to one of the most controversial areas of SA, whole-sequence comparison methods. Much of the SA literature in social sciences is devoted to introducing, evaluating, and discussing different approaches to comparing sequences by using either OM and its extensions (also called alignment-based methods) or alternative (non-alignment-based) methods. All of these approaches aim to measure the degree of dissimilarity between sequences. Calculating dissimilarities is a crucial step in identifying patterns among a set of sequences and thus is central to most SA applications. We start this chapter by introducing the classic optimal matching technique, a computational alignment procedure that quantifies the degree of dissimilarity of two sequences by evaluating how many data transformations are required to change one sequence into another. The transformation operations are associated with specific costs, and the dissimilarity between two sequences is given as the sum of the costs for aligning them. The specification of these costs is a very controversial issue that has been addressed in many methodological contributions since optimal matching was first introduced to social sciences. Reflecting this literature, the chapter covers several techniques of quantifying the pairwise dissimilarities between sequences using either optimal matching or other approaches. We discuss the substantial implications of the cost specification (e.g., focus on timing versus ordering of states); present different strategies for setting them (e.g., data-driven, based on state attributes, theory-driven); and compare the resulting outcomes using our example data. The computation of dissimilarities offers much room for analytical decisions on the part of the researcher, which often has been blamed as being a fundamental problem of SA. We agree that the analytical choices involved in the quantification of sequence resemblance can indeed be a critical step of SA, but we consider this a strength rather than a weakness of the method. The freedom of choice allows the researchers to make theoretically informed decisions that stress those attributes of the sequences—such as order, timing, or duration—they consider most important. In addition to the computation of full pairwise dissimilarity matrices that compare every sequence with every other sequence in the data set, Chapter 3 introduces techniques that compute pairwise dissimilarities among observed sequences and some sort of reference sequence. These reference sequences could correspond to a theoretically motivated sequence, the most prevalent or representative sequence, or the sequence of a significant other person (e.g., a sibling, parent, or partner). Contrary to the full comparison approach, this procedure usually yields only one dissimilarity value for every observation that can be further analyzed as an independent or dependent variable in some sort of regression analysis. For instance, in the context of a dyadic analysis, one could examine if the stability of a newly formed partnership is affected by the resemblance of the partners' previous partnership biographies, or figure out which dyadic characteristics decrease or increase the dissimilarity between two persons' previous partnership biographies.

Chapter 4 provides an overview and a thorough discussion of the most common analytical procedure succeeding the computation of a full pairwise sequence dissimilarity matrix, that is, cluster analysis. This method is employed to identify patterns among a set of sequences and assigns every sequence to a specific cluster. The chapter introduces and compares different clustering algorithms, presents techniques for evaluating the substantive quality of the clustering, and discusses heuristics for cluster validation. Finally, we will illustrate how regression analysis can be used to either predict the assignment to a specific cluster based on covariates measured prior to the beginning of the sequences or estimate the effects of cluster membership on an outcome measured at or after the end the sequences.

Chapter 5 is devoted to the analysis of multidimensional sequence data comprising information on multiple trajectories, such as employment, residential, and family biographies. With multichannel sequence analysis (MCSA), the SA toolkit offers a dedicated method for simultaneously analyzing multiple sequences that has steadily gained in popularity since its introduction by Gauthier and colleagues (Gauthier et al., 2010). Before turning to this approach, however, we discuss the potential and pitfalls of analyzing multiple trajectories simultaneously, introduce alternative approaches to handling multidimensional sequence data, and illustrate how to examine the statistical correlation of different sequence channels.

Chapter 6 introduces two procedures for studying the relationship between covariates and sequences that circumvent the step of cluster analysis: the discrepancy analysis framework and a procedure utilizing an adjusted version of the Bayesian information criterion. Drawing on well-established methods from the stochastic modeling culture, these two approaches avoid deterministic cluster assignment and allow for testing the relevance and statistical significance of group differences. The discrepancy framework proposed by Studer et al. (Studer et al., 2011) generalizes the principle of analysis of variance, while the approach of Liao and Fasang is introducing an adjusted version of the Bayesian information criterion and the likelihood ratio test (Liao & Fasang, 2021). We introduce and compare both approaches; show how they can be used to examine the association between sequences and multiple variables simultaneously; and demonstrate how the obtained results can be complemented by the implicative statistic (Studer, 2015), a simple test statistic that allows for visualizing how sequences differ across groups.

Chapter 7 delineates a selection of other, more recent approaches that bring together the stochastic and the algorithmic modeling cultures by combining either event history analysis or propensity score matching with SA (Barban et al., 2017; Studer, Liefbroer, & Mooyaart, 2018; Studer, Struffolino, & Fasang, 2018). Although it would go beyond this introductory book's scope to present these methods in detail, we consider it useful to point out these recent developments and refer the readers to the most relevant resources to further study these methods.

Chapter 8 concludes the book by summarizing important practical recommendations covering all analytical steps involved in typical sequence analysis projects.

1.3 Software, Data, and Companion Webpage

This book is targeted at persons who want to apply SA in their own research. Instead of lengthy discussions of theoretical and statistical foundations of SA,[1] it provides clear advice on how to apply various SA tools and raises awareness of the pitfalls related to the many analytical decisions involved in such an analysis. Against this background, we considered it useful to illustrate the procedures with a real-world data set comprising sequences on family formation as well as labor market participation. In a sense, these sequences are typical representatives for SA because much of

---

[1] For such discussions, the reader is referred to Abbott (2017), Abbott and Tsay (2000), Blanchard (2019), Cornwell (2015), Fasang and Mayer (2020), and Halpin (2014).

the applications and methodological contributions are related to the field of life course research. The data come from the German Family Panel (pairfam), release 10.0 (Brüderl et al., 2019). A description of the study can be found in Huinink et al. (2011). The data were collected between 2008 and 2018 and include detailed accounts on family and employment biographies. For the examples presented in the following chapters, we use data from a baseline sample of more than 4,000 respondents born between 1971 and 1973 for which we reconstructed sequences covering the age span of 18–40 years. The final analytical samples comprise 1,866 cases for the family biographies and 1,032 respondents for the labor market trajectories. Although we discuss the issue of missing data in Chapter 2, our example data include only sequences without any missing data or gaps along the sequences.

The companion webpage (https://sa-book.github.io) of this book hosts the data and code required for reproducing the results presented throughout the book. Next to plain code files, the companion page provides instructions and some bonus material introducing additional examples and analytical tools. The webpage also includes colored versions of the grayscale figures presented in this volume. Together with the book, these materials provide a comprehensive resource for self-study or use in methods courses on SA. In terms of software, the companion website provides material for the free software R. In R, the key packages for SA are TraMineR, TraMineRExtras (Gabadinho, Ritschard, Müller, & Studer, 2011), and WeightedCluster (Studer, 2013). Together they represent a very powerful and versatile environment for conducting SA.

Although the companion page will focus on R, we want to mention briefly the notable set of tools for conducting SA in Stata. Like in R, these tools are available in the form of user-written packages: SQ (Brzinsky-Fay et al., 2006), MICT (Halpin, 2016b, 2019), and SADI (Halpin, 2017). In most standard applications, both software environments are well suited for conducting SA and it is up to the user which program is preferred. That said, the material on the companion website uses R for several reasons: (a) Contrary to the commercial statistical software Stata, R is freely available; (b) the SA toolkit in R is much more encompassing, comprising many methods and functions that are not available in Stata; and (c) the development of new methods is taking place mainly within the R environment, making it the more future-proof choice.

CHAPTER 2

DESCRIBING AND VISUALIZING SEQUENCES

Before turning to numerical and graphical sequence description, this chapter introduces some basic concepts and definitions that are widely used in the sequence analysis (SA) literature and throughout this book. Note that this overview is selective in that it only covers concepts that are deemed relevant for the SA tools considered in later chapters. We will not, for instance, introduce the terminology of Markov models. Yet we will discuss most concepts and definitions that are pertinent to methods often applied in tandem with SA (e.g., cluster analysis, multinomial logistic regression, and event history analysis) in the respective chapters.

2.1 Basic Concepts and Terminology

Sequences are ordered lists of a discrete set of elements. In most social science applications, sequences are temporally ordered, but SA can also be applied to "timeless" sequences such as preference orders, cognitive schemas, or spatial orders (Cornwell, 2015). The set of elements constituting a sequence is called a state space or alphabet A. Following the notation of Elzinga and Liefbroer (2007), we can define a sequence x of length k as $x = x_1, x_2, \ldots x_k$ with $x_i \in A$ and i indicating the position of a state within the sequence x.

2.1.1 Sequences With Recurrent States

Most social science applications relate to *recurrent sequences*, where the elements of the alphabet can occur repeatedly in each sequence. Table 2.1 illustrates such sequences by presenting partnership trajectories of length $k = 6$. In our illustrative example of partnership biographies, the alphabet consists of the following states: single (S), living apart together (LAT), cohabiting (COH), and married (MAR).

Table 2.1   Example of two sequences

	x_1	x_2	x_3	x_4	x_5	x_6
Sequence A	S	S	LAT	COH	COH	MAR
Sequence B	COH	MAR	MAR	MAR	COH	COH

9

2.1.2 Episodes and Transitions

In both sequences shown in Table 2.1, certain states appear multiple times. A series of consecutively repeated states, such as *(S, S)* and *(MAR, MAR, MAR)*, is called an episode or spell. Note that even states that appear only once constitute episodes. According to this definition, Sequence A consists of four and Sequence B of three episodes.

Given the short length of the two example sequences, it is easy to recognize the episodes at a glance and it is possible to display the sequences in a table. Longer sequences call for more condensed notation. Our pairfam example data are particularly suitable to illustrate this point. The data provide monthly accounts of family formation and labor market participation biographies covering ages 18 to 40 years. The following example uses information on the respondents' partnership biographies applying the alphabet introduced earlier. This gives us recurrent sequences with a maximum of four different states and a length of $k = 22 \times 12 = 264$ months. A typical sequence can be written as follows:

LAT-LAT-LAT-LAT-LAT-LAT-LAT-LAT-LAT-LAT-LAT-LAT-LAT-S-S-S-S-
S-S-LAT-LAT-LAT-LATLAT-LAT-LAT-LAT-LAT-LAT-LAT-LAT-LAT-LAT-
LAT-LAT-LAT-LAT-LAT-LAT-LAT-LAT-LAT-LAT-LAT-LAT-LAT-LAT-
LAT-LAT-LAT-LAT-LAT-S-S-S-S-S-S-S-S-S-S-S-S-S-S-S-S-S-S-S-S-S-
S-S-LAT-LAT-LAT-LAT-LAT-LAT-LAT-LAT-LAT-LAT-LAT-LAT-LAT-
LAT-LAT-LAT-LAT-LAT-LAT-LAT-LAT-LAT-LAT-LAT-LAT-LAT-LAT-
LAT-LAT-LAT-LAT-LAT-LAT-LAT-LAT-LAT-LAT-LAT-LAT-LAT-LAT-S-
S-S-S-S-S-S-S-S-S-S-S-S-S-S-S-S-S-S-S-S-S-S-S-S-S-S-S-S-S-S-S-
S-LAT-LAT-LAT-LAT-LAT-LAT-LAT-LAT-LAT-LAT-COH-COH-COH-
COH-COH-COH-COH-COH-COH-COH-COH-COH-COH-COH-
MAR-MAR-MAR-MAR-MAR-MAR-MAR-MAR-MAR-MAR-MAR-
MAR-MAR-MAR-MAR-MAR-MAR-MAR-MAR-MAR-MAR-MAR-
MAR-MAR-MAR-MAR-MAR-MAR-MAR-MAR-MAR-MAR-MAR-
MAR-MAR-MAR-MAR-MAR-MAR-MAR-MAR-MAR-MAR-MAR-
MAR-MAR-MAR-MAR-MAR-MAR-MAR-MAR-MAR-MAR-MAR-
MAR-MAR-MAR-MAR-MAR-MAR-MAR-MAR-MAR-MAR-MAR-
MAR-MAR-MAR-MAR-MAR-MAR-MAR-MAR-MAR-MAR-MAR-
MAR-MAR-MAR-MAR-MAR-MAR-MAR-MAR-MAR-MAR-MAR

It is immediately evident that this notation, which is termed the state-sequence (STS) format, makes it difficult to identify episodes within sequences. This can be easily solved by listing only one distinct state for every episode:

LAT-S-LAT-S-LAT-S-LAT-COH-MAR

According to Gabadinho, Ritschard, Müller, and Studer (2011), this type of sequence representation is called distinct-successive-states (DSS) sequence format. It is an accessible account of the episodes and maintains the order of the original state sequence, but it lacks any information on the duration of the observed episodes. If the researcher's interest is only in the order of states, analyzing DSS sequences alone will suffice. In most applications, however, researchers are interested in the duration of episodes and the timing of events, and therefore want to utilize the full information stored in their data. Hence, avoiding the somewhat lengthy STS format, Aassve and colleagues (2007) have suggested the much more parsimonious state-permanence-sequence (SPS) notation, which is similar to the DSS format but also provides information about the length of a sequence's episodes by simply adding the duration of each episode. Thus, our example sequence would be as follows:

(LAT,13)-(S,6)-(LAT,33)-(S,24)-(LAT,41)-(S,35)-(LAT,10)-(COH,14)-(MAR,88)

As in DSS notation, here, it is easy to recognize the distinct episodes. Further, this notation shows that this 22-year-long sequence is clearly dominated by a marriage spell that lasted more than 7 years (88 months). The sequence also comprises two rather long LAT spells in the respondent's early and mid-twenties, each lasting roughly 3 years.

In addition to showing the episodes—which can be understood as building blocks of sequences—DSS and SPS notation also refer to another important concept in SA, namely, transitions. The example sequence comprises nine episodes; this implies that it includes eight transitions. The transitions from being single to LAT and from LAT to single occur three times each, while we observe only one transition to cohabitation and marriage. It is plausible to assume that the other sequences in the data show a similar pattern—that is, that "single" or "LAT" constitute origin or destination states of transitions considerably more often than "cohabitation" or "marriage." Likewise, we can expect similarities in terms of transition timing, with transitions in and out of LAT relationships mainly occurring in the early and mid-twenties and transitions to marriage coming in the late twenties or early thirties. The frequency and timing of transitions are not only interesting for deriving substantive insights into the process under study (see Section 2.3) but also relevant for data-driven approaches of measuring the similarity of sequences (see Chapter 3, Section 3.3) or assessing sequence complexity (see Section 2.5).

2.1.3 Subsequences

In addition to episodes and transitions, subsequences are another important component of sequences. According to Elzinga and Liefbroer (2007), a subsequence u of sequence x is defined as an ordered list in which the elements of alphabet A, that is, the set of categorical states constituting the sequence, appear in the same order as in sequence x (i.e., $u \subseteq x$). All sequences share two specific subsequences: the empty subsequence λ and the original sequence x. As a result, sequence $x = A, B, C$ already has eight distinct subsequences (λ; A; B; C; AB; AC; BC; ABC), which can be written as $\phi(x) = 8$.

Within the SA toolkit, subsequences are used to measure the degree of sequence turbulence (see Section 2.5) and for pairwise sequence comparisons (see Chapter 3, Section 3.4). Generally speaking, the more subsequences a sequence has, the more complex it is, and the more subsequences two sequences share, the more similar they are.

A Note on Data Formats

Sequence data come in a variety of formats. The most common ones—the wide, long, and spell data format—are depicted in the following table. Software packages for analyzing social science sequence data differ in their ability to work with different data formats. TraMineR is the most versatile package and is well suited for working with sequence data stored in the episode, long, or wide format. Stata's SQ (Brzinsky-Fay et al., 2006) requires the data to be stored in the long format, and SADI (Halpin, 2017) only works for sequence data stored in the wide format. Both R and Stata allow the data to be reshaped if it is not in the desired format (see companion webpage material for Chapter 2).

(a) Long format			(b) Wide format				(c) Episode/spell format				
id	obs.	x	id	x1	x2	x3	id	episode	x	start	end
1	1	A	1	A	A	B	1	1	A	1	2
1	2	A	2	B	C	C	1	2	B	3	3
1	3	B					2	1	B	1	1
2	1	B					2	2	C	2	3
2	2	C									
2	3	C									

2.2 Defining Sequences

As with all methods, the results of SA depend heavily on the researcher's analytical decisions. Being a rather new method, SA—and optimal matching in particular—has faced a lot of criticism since it was first introduced to the social sciences. Aisenbrey and Fasang (2010) have provided an excellent overview of the initial critique and subsequent methodological advances. Much of the early criticism was concerned with measuring similarity between sequences. Although this is indeed a critical step in many SA applications, the first analytical choices must already have been made when the data are actually being defined as sequences. More specifically, the researcher has to decide on the states that should be included in the alphabet, the point at which the sequences should begin and end, and the intervals at which the states should be measured; it is also necessary to determine how to deal with gaps, missing data, and sequences of unequal length. Unfortunately, there are no recipes for all of these analytical steps. Instead, the process is iterative and should be mainly guided by theoretical and substantive considerations. As a general heuristic, however, we recommend starting with a fine-grained analysis before turning to techniques that reduce the complexity in the data, such as collapsing rare states of the alphabet or aggregating monthly data into yearly data. In the following subsections, we discuss each of these analytical choices.

2.2.1 The Alphabet

The first analytical choice virtually always entails defining the alphabet (a.k.a. state space), that is, the set of categorical states that constitute the sequences. This step is largely determined by the data available to the researcher. In our example data on partnership biographies, for instance, the coding scheme allows us to distinguish between persons without a partner and persons who are in a partnership but are not cohabiting (LAT). Depending on the research question, this might be an important distinction, but it can rarely be made because many data sources only provide information on coresidential partnerships (Raab & Struffolino, 2019). Our data would have allowed for an even more extended alphabet that not only distinguished between different partnership states but also considered the partner with whom each state was experienced. Depending on the number of considered partnerships—the maximum number of partners p observed in pairfam is 14—this would result in a very extended alphabet (S, LAT$p1$, LAT$p2$, . . ., LAT$p14$, COH$p1$, . . ., COH$p14$, MAR$p1$, . . ., MAR$p14$) with sparsely occupied cells and arguably little potential for producing additional insights. This illustrates that a more nuanced alphabet is not necessarily conducive to a better analysis unless the research question calls for such a fine-grained specification.

Therefore, the main goal of the alphabet specification stage is to properly balance parsimony and detail. Many applications achieve this goal by collapsing categories if they occur rarely in the data or if they are considered irrelevant for theoretical reasons. In general, we consider this a reasonable strategy, because one of SA's main goals is to reduce complexity in order to enable the identification of relevant empirical regularities. Further, this strategy also acknowledges the limited capacity of human working memory, which makes it demanding and tedious to cognitively process large alphabets. Finally, the emphasis in SA on data visualization also favors small alphabets, because it becomes very difficult to come up with print-friendly qualitative color palettes that comprise more than nine states.

That said, we call for caution when lumping states together. While collapsing states ensures that the analyst does not lose sight of the most salient patterns hidden in complex data, it may obscure meaningful regularities that point to important minorities or deviant subgroups that warrant further consideration. We therefore recommend starting with a comprehensive state space and then testing whether this can be sensibly reduced based on substantive considerations regarding similarities between states. This implies an iterative process of sequence definition and further analysis, such as optimal matching and cluster analysis. Of course, this procedure should be guided by theoretical and substantive considerations.

If SA is applied to secondary data, the researcher's freedom to choose between different alphabet specifications is often extremely restricted and the differences in the results derived from diverse alphabets tend to be rather modest. The surprisingly weak impact of alphabet specification has even been shown with anthropological sequence data on figures in ritual dances, which leaves room for very divergent definitions of the coding scheme (Forrest & Abbott, 1990). The robustness of the results to changes in the alphabet can be assessed by inspecting the degree of resemblance of the dissimilarity matrices obtained by analyzing differently defined sequences. This can be achieved by inspecting the correlation of the matrices by calculating the Mantel coefficient or applying permutation tests for the similarity of matrices (Forrest & Abbott, 1990; Piccarreta, 2017; Piccarreta & Elzinga, 2013). We will illustrate these techniques in Chapter 5.

2.2.2 Sequence Length and Granularity

In previous sections, we broadly introduced sequences as ordered lists of (categorical) elements. In most applications, these lists are temporally ordered, which implies that sequences are defined with reference to some sort of time axis. Building on a classification suggested in the literature on event history analysis (Blossfeld & Rohwer, 2001), we distinguish between a calendar time axis or a process time axis. In the first setting, the beginning and end of the sequences are defined by a fixed time point, such as a specific year, chosen by the researcher. In the second scenario, the start of the sequence is defined by the occurrence of a specific event, such as a transition like leaving school or a specific birthday. Employment trajectories, for instance, are often set to begin once the respondents leave the school (Brzinsky-Fay, 2007; Struffolino, 2019). According to this definition, the sequences for some respondents might start at age 16 while for others they may begin 2 or 3 years later. This, of course, has important repercussions for any subsequent analysis and requires a constant awareness on the part of the analyst of the age differences of the analyzed sample. In many applications, the process time is defined by referring to a transition that marks the beginning of the observation period. In the second step, the analyst decides on the length of the respective observation period, such as the first 10 years after leaving school. Of course, sequences can also be defined with reference to their end date, such as entry into retirement or death (Raab et al., 2018).

The definition of the start and end dates and the granularity (measurement accuracy of the process time; e.g., measured in years, months, weeks, or days) of the available data determine the length of the sequences. For instance, the example sequences used in this book cover a period of 22 years (process time from age 18 to 40). Given that our data provide monthly information on status changes during this observation period, our sequences are of length $k = 22 \times 12 = 264$. Compared to most published social science studies using SA, these are rather long sequences. Even with our small alphabet of four different states, the data would allow for an overwhelming number of possible sequence realizations (i.e., $4^{264} \approx 8.79 \times 10^{185}$). Although researchers will observe only a fraction of this sequence universe, this data setting means they are very unlikely to observe the same sequence multiple times. Indeed, our example data of 1,866 cases contains 1,834 unique sequence realizations for partnership biographies.

This illustrates nicely how long sequences allow for extensive heterogeneity. As was also true when specifying large alphabets, the heterogeneity of long sequences is neither bad nor good when seeking to conduct a sound analysis. It is rather a question of what the analyst is interested in. Most SA applications aim at reducing complexity by searching for patterns. Accordingly, any analytical decisions made when specifying the sequences should be evaluated in light of this goal and the substantive question at hand. Some research questions call for nuance in order to identify rare regularities. In most applications, however, the goal is to uncover the most salient patterns hidden in the data. If this applies, the researcher should consider reducing the complexity when defining the sequences.

Turning back to our example, one could argue that it is not relevant to capture every single fleeting affair and that researchers should instead focus on serious relationships that last longer than a couple of months. In general, there are two approaches to reducing complexity in such a scenario:

1. *Data manipulation by recoding sequence states.* This data manipulation procedure should be based on a set of rules that is clearly communicated by the researcher. In our example, this strategy could be enacted by imposing a threshold rule that defines a minimum length for partnership spells. If a spell falls below this threshold value, it is discounted and the respective states coded as being single rather than in a relationship. Applying a threshold of 12 months as a minimum relationship duration only slightly reduces the number of distinct sequences from 1,834 to 1,787, but still leads to somewhat less complex sequences. Note that this recoding strategy is different from the one discussed in the previous section insofar as it does not alter the size of the alphabet.

2. *Reduction of the sequence length by aggregation.* Unlike the first approach, this strategy entails both a substantive and a structural change in the sequence data, because it reduces sequence length. Executing this technique requires a rule specifying how the data should be aggregated. A predefined number of adjacent states (e.g., 12 months) can be summarized according to the first, the last, or the most frequently observed state. In the SA literature, the process of aggregating successive positions is sometimes referred to as changing the time granularity of sequences. Applying this strategy to our example data, we aggregated monthly to yearly data using each year's modal value. This reduced the sequence length from 264 to 22 and the number of distinct sequences from 1,834 to 1,432, although the observation window still covered the same time period as before.

In simplifying the original data, neither approach fully utilizes the available information; they should thus be applied with some caution. In general, the second strategy is more invasive and has a greater impact on further analysis. It also reduces the computing load and is therefore particularly suitable for large data sets and lengthy sequences with complex alphabets. Table 2.2 illustrates how the two approaches modify the original data for a subset of our partnership sequences.

17

Table 2.2 Comparison of different approaches toward defining sequence
data

Initial sequence (states affected by the data reduction techniques printed in boldface)	Strategy 1: recode (only considers partnerships lasting at least 1 year)	Strategy 2: aggregate (monthly to yearly data using modal values)
(S,89)-(LAT,26)-(COH,14)- **(LAT,6)**-*(S,34)*-**(LAT,4)**- *(MAR,91)*	*(S,89)-(LAT,26)- (COH,14)-(S,44)- (MAR,91)*	*(S,7)-(LAT,3)-(COH,1)- (S,3)-(MAR,8)*
(LAT,13)-(S,6)-(LAT,33)- (S,24)-(LAT,41)-(S,35)- (LAT,10)-(COH,14)- (MAR,88)	*(LAT,13)-(S,6)- (LAT,33)-(S,24)- (LAT,41)-(S,45)- (COH,14)-(MAR,88)*	*(LAT,1)-(S,1)-(LAT,2)- (S,2)-(LAT,4)-(S,3)- (LAT,1)-(COH,1)- (MAR,7)*
(S,56)-(LAT,69)-(COH,47)- (MAR,92)	*(S,56)-(LAT,69)- (COH,47)- (MAR,92)*	*(S,5)-(LAT,5)-(COH,4)- (MAR,8)*
(LAT,4)-*(S,134)*-**(LAT,9)**- **(COH,3)**-*(MAR,52)*- **(LAT,5)**-*(COH,25)*- *(MAR,32)*	*(S,150)-(MAR,52)- (S,5)-(COH,25)- (MAR,32)*	*(S,12)-(MAR,5)- (COH,2)-(MAR,3)*

Because it changes the granularity of the data, the second approach has greater potential to reduce the complexity of the original data. Apart from the sequence depicted in the last row of Table 2.2, however, the results obtained by the two strategies are surprisingly similar, although the sequence data structure of the approaches varies considerably ($k = 264$ vs. $k = 22$). Both approaches tend to reduce the number of LAT spells, because these relationships are characterized by short durations. Otherwise, the manipulated data are pretty similar to the original data and the changes are much less severe than might be expected. To give a comparison, changing the alphabet by recoding LAT relationships to being single would affect the sequences much more.

2.2.3 Sequences of Unequal Length: Censoring and Missing Data

The examples considered up to this point only include sequences of equal length. In a few cases, the fact that some realizations of the same process are of different durations is an empirical finding that can be relevant to specific research questions: For example, when looking at the timing of democratization, and accounting for prior political regimes' histories, one of the outcomes of interest may be the very fact that countries differ with regard to the length of the democratization process (Wilson, 2014). Another example is coming from the survey methodology literature, which is increasingly analyzing paradata capturing information about field processes. These data comprise information on contact histories of unequal length summarizing the number, timing, and outcome of contact attempts. Recent applications have analyzed these process data using SA to gain valuable insight for improving survey monitoring and survey management (Kreuter & Kohler, 2009).

In the vast majority of the cases, however, the SA literature consists of studies that use data in which each unit of analysis is observed for the same period and the sequences do not have any missing value. This is not because the data are free of missing values; rather, it points to the absence of well-established ways of working with missing or censored data in SA (Cornwell, 2015; Piccarreta & Studer, 2018). For this reason, most studies do one of the following: They replace gaps with valid values using some sort of imputation, add an additional missing state to the alphabet, or delete cases with missing data.

In general, there are two sources of missing values in sequences: censoring and gaps. Sequences are censored if not every unit of analysis was observed for the same time period. This is a typical scenario for panel studies, in which respondents often enter and leave the survey at different time points. While censoring pertains to the boundaries of sequences, missing values also manifest as gaps surrounded by valid information. In surveys, this is usually the result of temporary item or unit nonresponse. Simply abandoning the missing states would result in sequences of unequal length. Although the SA toolkit provides techniques for normalizing sequence distances, this is not a viable strategy for dealing with sequences of unequal length (Elzinga & Studer, 2019). A strategy of replacing missing values with a dedicated missing state in the alphabet also cannot be recommended. Although this produces sequences of equal length, it hampers subsequent analysis. In pairwise sequence comparisons, for instance, sequences sharing many missing states would be considered similar, although the missing category is only a placeholder for all states of the alphabet (Piccarreta & Studer, 2018).

Halpin (2016a) has proposed a technical solution to this problem. Instead of treating missing states as identical, he introduced the notion of "non-self-identical" missing values. According to this approach, sequences that share many missing values are regarded as being dissimilar to each other, which is much more plausible in most applications than the assumption that they are similar.

Imputation techniques are another promising approach to handling missing values. One common method for dealing with gaps can be applied in the data manipulation stage of the analysis. Here, the researcher simply defines a set of rules to close gaps in the data. In our partnership biographies, for instance, if there was a gap of 5 months surrounded by two single episodes, it could be closed by imputing the state single. If there was a gap surrounded by different states, both states could be used to close the gap in a symmetric fashion. Yet, this strategy might result in underestimating the true volatility of sequences by simply replacing the missing states with the surrounding states, although the gap could actually point to one or multiple episodes spent in a different state. From a statistical point of view, this kind of data imputation is based on strong assumptions as it does not reflect the uncertainty about the imputed values. It simply assumes that the real values are known.

A statistically correct alternative requires multiple imputations for each missing observation. Multiple imputation techniques are widely available in the most commonly used statistical software packages but mainly refer to the imputation of cross-sectional data. Halpin (2016b) has proposed a tweaked imputation procedure specifically tailored for use with categorical time series data. The algorithm fills the elements of the gap successively by using the first valid values surrounding a missing state. In this stepwise procedure, the technique uses values that have already been imputed to predict the remaining missing values. Halpin has provided a dedicated software package for Stata, named MICT, that facilitates the application of his ideas. He has also tested how his imputation procedure compares to the alternative imputation procedures in a simulation scenario with a random missing pattern (missing at random = MAR). The results obtained by MICT tend to perform better in retaining the "longitudinal consistency" of the sequence data than traditional multiple imputation, multiple imputation by chained equations, or the more recently proposed two-fold fully conditional specification (Nevalainen et al., 2009) for imputing missing values in longitudinal data. MICT, however, is currently unable to include additional variables with missing values in the imputation model. This is a major drawback because standard imputation techniques call for a joint imputation of all missing values of the variables used in the analysis. Given that SA is virtually always applied in tandem with other multivariable methods, the occurrence of additional missing values is very likely, and analysts must rely on more established imputation procedures, despite the fact that MICT is arguably better suited for sequence data.

An additional problem arises if the dissimilarity matrices retrieved by analyzing multiple imputed sequence data should be examined further by some sort of cluster analysis. Contrary to regression analysis, multiple imputation is rarely applied in the context of cluster analysis, and the literature still lacks well-established guidelines on how to proceed in such a case (see Basagaña et al., 2013, for some recommendations). In sum, the handling of missing data in SA remains a problem that warrants further research. Given the lack of clear guidelines, most SA applications still pertain to the analysis of completely observed sequences and try to close gaps in the data manipulation stage of the project rather than in the context of a statistically sound imputation procedure.

2.3 Description of Sequence Data I: The Basics

A sound sequence analysis is based on a good descriptive understanding of the analyzed data. The basic description of sequence data does not require specific techniques as it mainly provides counts and averages of different sequence properties.

2.3.1 Time Spent In Different States and Occurrence of Episodes

An overview of the average time spent in the different states of the alphabet as well as the average number of state-specific episodes is a good starting point for describing the data. Using the monthly example data on partnership trajectories, Table 2.3 shows that the respondents in the sample spend 36% of the time in marriages (95 of 264 months), while the corresponding figures for time spent in LAT relationships or coresidential unions are only half as high. Time spent outside relationships ranks between these two extremes. Although the respondents spent the shortest amount of time in LAT relationships, the corresponding number of episodes is (slightly) higher than for the other states. People experience more than twice as many LAT spells than marriage episodes (1.8 vs. 0.8) but spend only half the time in these partnerships, suggesting comparatively short average durations of approximately 2 years per LAT relationship.

2.3.2 Transition Rates

Once the average number of distinct episodes is known, the obvious next step is the examination of transitions between episodes and states. In the monthly sequence data, the average number of transitions is 4.3, whereas the same figure for the yearly data equals 3.3.

Moving beyond simple averages, transition rates between consecutive time points can provide even more insight into how the sequences unfold. In most social science applications, however, sequences are characterized by a considerable amount of stability. This means that most individuals do

Table 2.3 Average time spent in different states and number of spells

State	Time spent in state x in months			Number of episodes	
	Mean	SD	Rel. freq.	Mean	SD
S	72.5	69.8	0.27	1.6	1.2
LAT	48.0	43.9	0.18	1.8	1.3
COH	48.6	53.3	0.18	1.0	0.8
MAR	95.0	78.9	0.36	0.8	0.5

not change their status between two observations of a categorical time series. Using sequence data of a finer granularity, such as monthly versus yearly data, further contributes to a low share of transitions between states. As a result, transition matrices for sequence data with recurrent states often are not very informative apart from demonstrating the salience of the concept of path dependency.

For instance, the transition rates of both the monthly and yearly sequence data depicted in Table 2.4 show that only a (small) minority of people change their partnership status between two consecutive observations. That being said, the table also illustrates that coding the sequences with a yearly granularity produces slightly more interesting results. While for the monthly data, virtually all transitions are recorded on the main diagonal—indicating stability in partnership status from one month to the next—the yearly data reveal more transitions between consecutive observations. Particularly in the case of LAT relationships, the transition matrix corroborates earlier findings on the rather temporary nature of this type of partnership by demonstrating that 32% of persons in LAT relationships are observed in a different status 1 year later. While 12% of these LAT relationships end in separation, 20% are further institutionalized, either as coresidential unions (16%) or marriages (4%).

Examining the transition rates of sequences stored in the DSS format can provide further insights by removing recurrent appearances of the same state in consecutive positions of the sequence. A transition matrix based on this format provides transition rates between episodes of distinct states. Accordingly, the cells on the diagonal equal zero. By definition, this approach yields higher transition rates between different states compared to the previous procedure, even with data of fine granularity.

The transition matrix for the monthly DSS sequence data shown in Table 2.5 illustrates this point well. Interestingly, this matrix shows that more than half

Table 2.4 Transition matrix of sequences stored in STS format

State at t	State at $t+1$							
	Monthly granularity				Yearly granularity			
	S	LAT	COH	MAR	S	LAT	COH	MAR
S	0.98	0.02	0.00	0.00	0.81	0.14	0.04	0.01
LAT	0.02	0.96	0.02	0.00	0.12	0.68	0.16	0.04
COH	0.00	0.00	0.98	0.01	0.04	0.02	0.80	0.14
MAR	0.00	0.00	0.00	1.00	0.01	0.01	0.00	0.98

Table 2.5 Transition matrix of sequences stored in DSS format

State at t	State at $t+1$			
	S	LAT	COH	MAR
S	0.00	0.91	0.07	0.02
LAT	0.42	0.00	0.50	0.08
COH	0.20	0.12	0.00	0.68
MAR	0.44	0.46	0.11	0.00

(57%) of those whose marriages ended swiftly moved on to the next relationship without an intermediate single episode. When interpreting these results, one should be aware that the analysis of DSS transition matrices only examines *movers*, because all *stayers* are removed from the data.

2.3.3 State Distribution and Shannon Entropy At Different Positions

Although the tools introduced earlier build a strong descriptive foundation, they are limited in the sense that they only produce aggregate indicators summarizing entire sequences without providing information on how these sequences develop across time.[1] The inspection of the state

---

[1] Although it would be possible to calculate transition matrices or other measures at different positions of the sequences, we do not consider this a very promising approach. The transition rates at different positions, for instance, are usually very low if the sequence length is not very small. In addition, and particularly in the case of long sequences, the transition rates at a specific position—such as from month 126 to 127—are not very meaningful from a substantive point of view.

Table 2.6 State distribution at selected positions

State	Age						
	18	20	24	28	32	36	40
S	0.65	0.52	0.36	0.25	0.18	0.15	0.14
LAT	0.31	0.32	0.25	0.17	0.12	0.10	0.05
COH	0.03	0.11	0.23	0.25	0.22	0.15	0.13
MAR	0.01	0.05	0.17	0.33	0.48	0.60	0.68

distribution at different positions of the sequence addresses this limitation. Table 2.6 displays the distribution of partnership states at ages 18, 20, 24, 28, 32, 36, and 40. The table reveals that until their late 20s, most respondents report that they are currently without a partner. While singles remain a notable minority until the end of the sequences, marriage becomes the modal, or most prevalent, state at this age, and two thirds of the respondents indicate that they are married at age 40.

Table 2.7 complements these figures by describing the heterogeneity of the respective distributions using Shannon entropy. The entropy index S is defined as

$$S = -\sum_{i=1}^{a} p_i \times \log(p_i)$$

where p_i denotes the proportion of cases in state i and a is the size of the alphabet (Gabadinho, Ritschard, Müller, & Studer, 2011). At a given position of the sequence, S equals 1 when each state of the alphabet is observed equally often and 0 when only one state is observed.

Table 2.7 Shannon entropy at selected positions

	Age						
	18	20	24	28	32	36	40
Entropy	0.58	0.78	0.97	0.98	0.9	0.8	0.69

For our example data, the inversely u-shaped pattern of the entropy values substantiates the results reported in Table 2.7. The heterogeneity in the state distribution is lowest at age 18 and increases until the respondents are in their late 20s before it decreases again.

Before turning to the visualization of sequences, a word of caution regarding the interpretation of state distributions is in order. State distributions depict aggregated cross-sectional snapshots at different positions of the sequence. They do not convey any direct information on how individual sequences unfold across time. In the monthly partnership sequences, for instance, an inspection of the state distributions across all positions of the sequence indicates that the share of singles never falls below 13%. A thorough longitudinal inspection of the individual biographies, however, reveals that the share of persons who never experienced a partnership episode is less than 1%.

2.3.4 Modal and Representative Sequences

Some SA applications draw on the state distribution to report the modal sequence, that is, a sequence composed of the most prevalent states at each position of the sequence. In accordance with the results reported earlier, this sequence comprises only two of the four partnership states. Written in SPS notation, the sequence of modal states derived from the monthly state distributions is *(S,102)-(MAR,162)*. Note that the modal sequence is of limited use because it is virtually always a hypothetical sequence based on aggregated cross-sectional state distributions that is not actually observed in the data.

Therefore, we recommend other approaches for identifying those sequences that best represent the data. These techniques are based on a matrix measuring the pairwise dissimilarities between sequences. Chapter 3 introduces several different approaches for computing such dissimilarity matrices. Since there are a number of different takes on measuring sequence dissimilarities, the identification of a set of representative sequences hinges on the chosen dissimilarity measure. For now, however, it suffices to understand that a dissimilarity matrix allows differentiating sequences that are (very) dissimilar to the remaining sequences in the data from those that are more central, that is, less dissimilar to the other sequences.

After obtaining the dissimilarity matrix, the identification of a set of representative sequences requires additional analytical choices. The analyst has to decide how many representative sequences should be extracted from the universe of observed sequences as well as which representativeness criterion should be used for the extraction. Based on these decisions, the algorithm identifies a subset of nonredundant sequences in an iterative procedure.

Table 2.8 displays a set of representative sequences using the example data on yearly partnership biographies. These sequences were extracted by applying the neighborhood density criterion. According to this criterion,

Table 2.8 Set of representative sequences

Sequence	Coverage	Assigned
(S,1)-(LAT,2)-(MAR,19)	5.7	6.5
(S,20)-(MAR,2)	4.4	25.2
(S,4)-(LAT,1)-(COH,1)-(MAR,16)	3.8	5.3
(LAT,3)-(COH,2)-(MAR,17)	3.1	11.4
(S,2)-(LAT,2)-(COH,3)-(MAR,15)	2.7	17.1
(S,5)-(LAT,2)-(COH,2)-(MAR,13)	2.7	23.5
(COH,2)-(MAR,20)	2.6	3.0
(S,1)-(LAT,5)-(MAR,16)	2.3	8.0
Total Coverage	27.5	100.0

sequences are considered neighbors if their pairwise dissimilarity falls below a predefined threshold value—in this case, 10% of the maximum possible distance value. The share of neighboring sequences indicates the coverage of a sequence. We aimed at identifying a subset of nonredundant representative sequences with a total coverage of at least 25%. This criterion was met after the extraction of eight sequences.[2] The coverage of the first sequence depicted in Table 2.6 amounts to 5.7%. This means that every 20th person in our data set is described accurately by a sequence comprising a very short period without a partner *(S,1)* followed by a short LAT spell *(LAT,2)*, which is converted into a stable marriage *(MAR,19)* already in the early 20s. Given that marriage was the modal state in the second half of the sequences, it comes as no surprise that all representative sequences end in marriages. That said, the table reveals a considerable level of variability in the pathways leading to this predominant destination state. Contrary to the first sequence, for instance, the second representative sequence is characterized by a very long single spell *(S,20)*.

---

[2] Note that the representative sequences in Table 2.8 are sorted by coverage, whereas the algorithm extracted the sequences in a different order. As a result, the representative extracted last had a coverage of 2.7%, leading to a total coverage exceeding the threshold of 25% by 2.7 percentage points.

Note that the algorithm assigns every sequence in the data set to its closest representative even if the respective sequence does not meet the predefined representativeness criterion. As a result, the share of sequences assigned to a specific representative usually exceeds the share of sequences that are covered by it (see Table 2.8). High discrepancies between the two values often suggest that many of the assigned sequences are not characterized that well by their representative. TraMineR provides more sophisticated quality measurements than this simple visual inspection. For a detailed discussion of the identification and assessment of representative sequences, see the comprehensive introduction by Gabadinho, Ritschard, Studer, and Müller (2011).

This section clearly demonstrated that representative sequences are a more complex but also a much more useful tool for exploring and summarizing a large body of sequences compared to presenting a simple sequence of modal states. While we used this tool for tabular description, most applications use it to graphically illustrate sequence data—particularly if the data comprise too many cases to plot all sequences without visual artifacts (see Fasang & Liao, 2014, and Section 2.4.2 on relative frequency sequence plots in this chapter). Moreover, representative sequences are not usually extracted for the full data set but only for different subgroups, for instance, groups obtained after OM and cluster analysis or substantively interesting subpopulations, such as persons with different educational attainment or ethnic origin.

In doing so, many applications report only one single representative per group, the so-called *medoid sequence*. The medoid is defined as the most central object of a given subset of sequences, that is, it has the lowest sum of dissimilarities to all other sequences. Comparing the medoid partnership trajectory of women—*(S,3)-(LAT,2)-(COH,4)-(MAR,13)*; coverage = 3.4—to men's medoid sequences—*(S,7)-(LAT,4)-(COH,3)-(MAR,8)*; coverage = 1—shows that the most notable differences occur at the beginning and the end of the observational window. Compared to the "medoid woman," the "medoid man" remains single for 4 additional years during early adulthood and marries 5 years later.

2.4 Visualization of Sequences

The tabular inspection of sequences conveys a lot of information that can easily become hard to interpret for both the analyst and the recipients. This is due to the high level of complexity of sequence data, which arises from the categorical level of the measurement of sequences and from repeated measurements per unit of analysis. Contrary to cross-sectional numerical data, sequences cannot be satisfactorily summarized by presenting the mean or the standard deviation of a single numerical indicator such as income. Instead, a thorough description requires the exploration of the distribution of multiple categorical states at different positions of the sequence (see Tables 2.6 and 2.7) as well as the inspection of sequence-specific composite measures. As a result, the tabular description of sequence data runs the risk of producing an overwhelming number of figures that, despite their accuracy, hamper the recognition of regularities in which the researcher is actually interested.

In view of this limitation, this chapter explores how graphical tools can complement the tabular description and demonstrates that they are frequently capable of communicating the same level of information in a more efficient and effective manner (Healy & Moody, 2014; Tufte, 1983). Visualization has played a prominent role in the SA literature since the proliferation of dedicated software packages for Stata and R, and recent contributions constitute notable additions to the visualization toolkit (Bürgin & Ritschard, 2014; Fasang & Liao, 2014; Piccarreta, 2012). This section presents a small selection of those tools that we consider most useful and that figure most prominently in the applied SA literature. We mainly draw on the excellent overviews provided by Brzinsky-Fay (2014) and Fasang and Liao (2014), to which we also refer for more detailed coverage of sequence visualization.

Following Fasang and Liao (2014), we distinguish two groups of graphs for sequence visualization. *Data summarization graphs* (Section 2.4.1) aggregate and summarize the information stored in the sequences. These graphs visualize one or two dimensions of information stored in sequence data (Brzinsky-Fay, 2014) by presenting the different categories of the alphabet and providing some information on the (temporal) order of the observed states. *Data representation graphs* (Section 2.4.2) add a third layer of information by plotting individual sequences rather than only aggregated summary measures. As a result, they are richer in information but also more demanding for the viewer.

Using colors to depict the different states of the alphabet can simplify the interpretation of complex sequence graphs considerably. Although the increase in electronic publishing in recent years has contributed to the widespread use of colored figures, printing costs sometimes still prohibit the use of color in print outlets. Due to this common restriction, we illustrate how one might visualize sequence data in grayscale. While it is possible to produce most of the figures in grayscale, we recommend using color figures whenever possible. For guidance on choosing appropriate colors, see the contributions by Zeileis and colleagues (Zeileis et al., 2009; Zeileis et al., 2019). The companion website at **https://sa-book.github.io** provides further details on using predefined and optimized color palettes for visualizing sequences using HCL color palettes.

A Note on Grayscale Figures

Visualizing sequences in grayscale rather than in different colors restricts the options available to the analyst. Palettes of gray—like the one depicted in the following figure—are sequential palettes.

That is, they suggest that the data convey some sort of ordinal information. SA applications, however, often work with categorical alphabets, and the notion of a hierarchy between states might result in distorted visualizations.

Although the alphabet of partnership states analyzed in this book is also categorical, one could impose a hierarchy reflecting the partnership's degree of institutionalization (Single < LAT < Cohabitation < Marriage). Accordingly, the usage of a sequential palette of grays does not present much of a problem for this specific application. This is also true because the alphabet comprises only four different states. If the number of categories exceeds this level, gray palettes run the risk of becoming unsuitable for printing. Yet in some applications, the addition of shading lines might be a viable option for producing high-quality grayscale visualizations when facing larger alphabets. The following example and figure are a good illustration of this approach. The initial alphabet of four partnership states is extended by adding information on the parental status of the respondents. For each partnership state, we distinguish between childless persons and parents. For married persons, we add even more nuance by differentiating parents with one child from parents with multiple children. This results in an alphabet of nine different states, which can be visualized by four "colors" (white and three shades of gray) depicting the partnership states and by shading lines indicating the parental status.

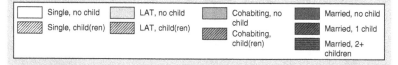

The companion website features detailed instructions on how to produce such a grayscale color palette in R.

The following sections complement Section 2.3 by presenting graphs corresponding to the tables presented earlier. If not indicated differently, the plots are based on the monthly partnership data. Except for the transition plot, which was made using the ggplot2 package (Wickham, 2016), all figures were generated with the TraMineR package's visualization functions.

2.4.1 Data Summarization Graphs

Transition Plot

The transition plots in Figure 2.1 are based on transition matrices of yearly partnership data (see Table 2.4) using sequences stored in two different formats. The left panel is based on STS sequence data and therefore is dominated by high values on the main diagonal that indicate that even in modern societies, people rarely change their partnership status on a monthly basis. The right panel is based on DSS sequence data that do not allow for subsequent repetitions of the same state. Accordingly, the plot visualizes how the outflow transitions are distributed among the four partnership states.

Figure 2.1 Two transition plots of yearly partnership sequences

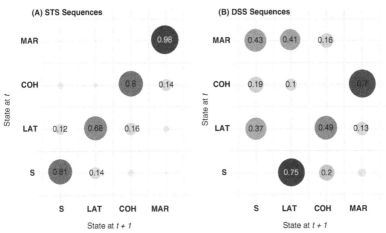

The size of the circles and the intensity of the gray shading increase with the prevalence of transitions between the two depicted states. If the share of outflow transitions in a given row reaches a threshold of 10%, the circles are labeled accordingly. Compared to the tabular presentation, this kind of plot emphasizes the most prevalent transitions. Note, however, that neither the transition matrices nor the transition plots provide any information on how many persons experience each transition. Similarly, it remains unclear when the transitions are taking place because the reported transition rates are averaged across all positions of the sequences. Screen presentations allow the researcher to address this issue by rendering transition plots at different positions of the sequences and displaying them sequentially, for example, as an animated GIF file (see companion website for an illustration).

Modal State Plot

In Section 2.3, we identified the modal sequence $(S,102)$-$(MAR,162)$ for the entire sample of the example data. Without further information, the modal sequence contributes little to the understanding of the underlying data. Therefore, we strongly recommend adding a graphical depiction of the relative frequencies of the modal states at each position of the sequence.

Figure 2.2 demonstrates the added value of such an illustration. The figure not only displays the modal sequences for men and women, it also shows how the numerical dominance of the modal state(s) varies across sequence positions. For instance, in addition to showing that marriage is the modal state for women and men in their 30s, the figure also reveals that the dominance of this modal state is much more pronounced for women. Two thirds of the women are already married in their mid-30s, whereas the corresponding numbers for men never reach such a high level. Moreover, the plots show that the modal states at the beginning and the end of the sequences are more dominant, whereas the phase in between is characterized by more volatility—particularly for women.

State Distribution Plot

The state distribution plot (for an early application, see Blossfeld, 1987) represents the natural extension of the modal state plot. Technically speaking, it visualizes the distribution of all states by plotting a series of stacked bar charts at each position of the sequence. Figure 2.3 represents two state distribution plots using sequence data on family formation with yearly and monthly granularity ($k = 22$ vs. $k = 264$). Compared to the modal plot, Figure 2.3 provides additional insights by also displaying the distribution of the nonmodal states and using an enlarged alphabet that incorporates information on the parenthood status. At age 40, for instance, roughly half of the nonmarrieds are already parents.

Figure 2.2 Modal state plots for women and men

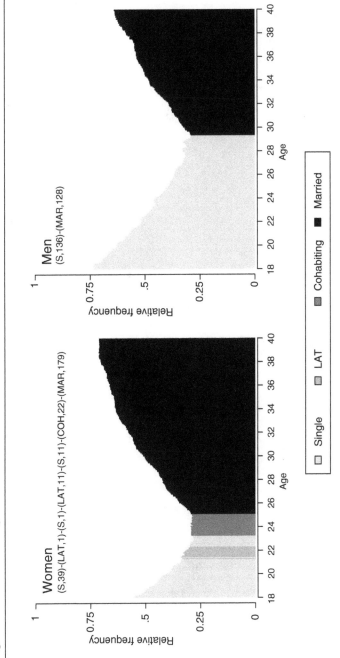

Figure 2.3 State distribution plots with different levels of granularity

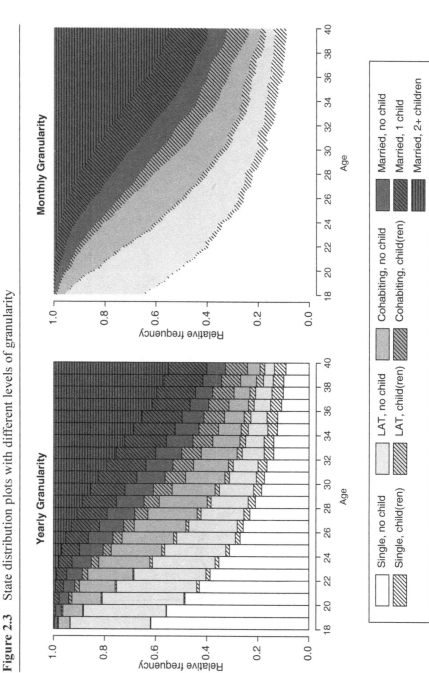

Although the aggregated yearly data are less accurate, they do not change the interpretation of the results. Based on the similarity of results and the fact that the yearly data are less demanding from a computational point of view, this figure can be interpreted to support using the yearly data for further analyses. That said, we recommend such an approach without reservations only if hardware restrictions make this necessary.

Concluding the section on summarization graphs, Figure 2.4 shows a slightly enhanced version of the standard state distribution plot that also includes information on the state entropy at the different positions of the sequences. Note, however, that we only recommend this type of visualization for displaying sequences with small alphabets; hence, the figure is focusing on the partnership trajectories and neglects the information on parenthood status. The gender-specific entropy distributions point to notable differences. While the general pattern is the same for men and women, the plots reveal differences in the temporal shape and the level of entropy. Among males, for example, the entropy at the end of the observation period exceeds the initial entropy at age 18. By contrast, the entry and exit levels of entropy among women seem to be very similar.

2.4.2 Data Representation Graphs

The previous section illustrated a variety of approaches toward visualizing summary statistics of sequence data. Although the presented figures provide valuable information in an accessible fashion, they lose sight of how individual sequences unfold and thus are not well suited for uncovering and visualizing groups of similar sequences. Moreover, figures and tables of aggregated data must be interpreted with caution in order to avoid the risk of committing the ecological fallacy. This is nicely illustrated in Figure 2.5, which shows three visualizations based on two constructed data sets, each comprising 10 sequences of length $k = 5$.

Next to a state distribution plot, the figure displays two sequence index plots. In the latter, each horizontally stacked bar represents one individual sequence. Although the sequences are sorted by the first occurrence of the partnership status "married," the index plots are visually less structured than the state distribution plot in the left panel of the figure. Communicating a higher amount of information (i.e., actual individual sequences) comes at the price of more visual complexity. The two index plots literally represent the full data, while the distribution plot summarizes them. The left panel of Figure 2.5 shows that the two very different samples of sequences can be summarized by one single state distribution plot. If the distribution plot is accurately interpreted, this does not pose a problem. For instance, the distribution plot shows neither that 20% of the observed

Figure 2.4 State distribution plots and entropy by gender

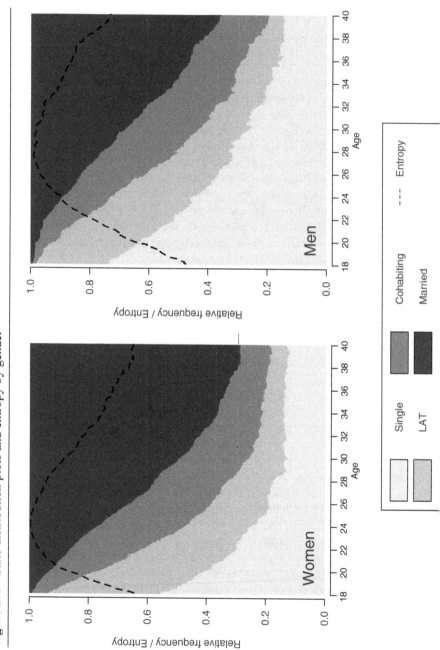

Figure 2.5 Different data producing the same state distribution plot

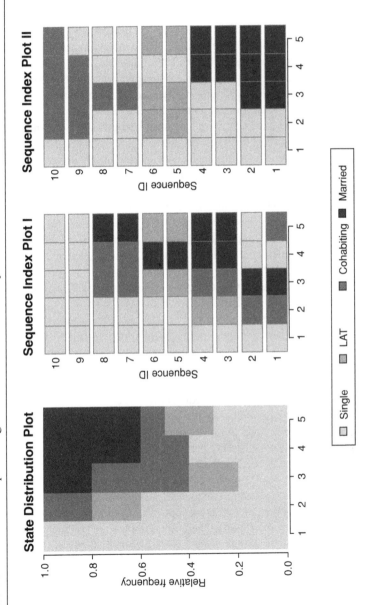

persons are permanently single nor that 60% never marry. Instead, it depicts that at every position of the sequences at least 20% currently do not have a partner and that 40% of the sample is married at the sequences' two final positions. The two index plots demonstrate that this aggregate picture can be brought about by two distinct populations. In the first sample, 80% of the individuals are married at some point. In the second sample, not a single case stays without a partner throughout the entire observation period.

By fully displaying the sequences, index plots are a valuable explorative visual tool for detecting structure in sequence data (Brzinsky-Fay, 2014). The accuracy and usefulness of index plots, however, hinge on the complexity of the visualized data. If the alphabet becomes too large, the resulting graph is difficult to decipher, particularly if the use of color is not an option. Keeping an eye on the number of plotted observations is an even more significant issue than the size of the alphabet. If too many sequences are displayed in one index plot, the issue of overplotting arises. That is, due to a lack of space in the plot region the stacked bars (or lines) depicting the individual sequences are partly plotted on top of each other and thus produce an inaccurate representation of the data. Depending on the plot size, overplotting arises if more than 300 to 400 sequences are displayed in one plot (Brzinsky-Fay, 2014).

The problem can be alleviated slightly by sorting the sequences such that similar sequences are plotted next to (and partly on top of) each other, rather than in the order they appear in the data set. This is not a satisfactory solution, though, because overplotting of (similar) sequences still occurs. Thus, reducing the number of plotted sequences is a more promising approach. This can be achieved by applying different strategies such as plotting (a) the most frequent sequences, (b) a random sample of sequences, or (c) a sample of representative sequences.

The first strategy is viable only if a few sequences represent a large share of the data, which is rarely the case in social science applications. Even our yearly sequence data of 1,866 partnership trajectories with a moderate sequence length of $k = 22$ and an alphabet with only four different states already comprises 1,432 unique sequences. Therefore, the second strategy, plotting a random selection of sequences, usually produces a more representative visualization of the sequences. The sampling, however, might distort the visualization slightly. Therefore, sampling and plotting should be applied repeatedly to estimate the extent of potential misrepresentation (Brzinsky-Fay, 2014).

Instead of visualizing random samples of the data, more sophisticated strategies aim at extracting and plotting only those sequences that represent the data best. According to Fasang and Liao (2014), some of these approaches, such as representative sequence plots (Gabadinho, Ritschard,

Studer, & Müller, 2011) or the smoothing techniques suggested by Piccarreta (2012) try to improve the visualization of sequences by either removing redundant information or plotting only the most relevant sequences. Taking a different approach, relative frequency sequence plots, developed by Fasang and Liao (2014), aim at reducing visual complexity and the problem of overplotting while maintaining an accurate representation of the data across the full spectrum of observed sequences. This goal is achieved by the following procedure.

First, the sequences are sorted according to a substantively meaningful principle such as the timing of a specific transition (e.g., age at first marriage) or the score on the first factor obtained by multidimensional scaling (MDS) of a dissimilarity matrix (Piccarreta & Lior, 2010). In our experience, the latter sorting strategy often produces better results, although the quality heavily depends on the chosen dissimilarity measure (see Chapter 3).

Although regular index plots are considerably improved by sorting the sequences, the order of sequences is even more critical in the context of sequence frequency plots. In regular sequence index plots, initially introduced by Scherer (2001), sorting eases the recognition of patterns without changing what is displayed. That is, irrespective of the sorting order, all sequences are rendered. In relative frequency index plots, however, the rendered medoids and the goodness of fit of the plot differ depending on the sorting order (see companion page for an example).

Once the data are sorted, they are divided into k similarly sized frequency groups. The next step extracts the medoid sequence for each of these groups. The resulting sample of k medoid sequences is rendered in an index plot. The index plot can be complemented by box-and-whisker plots, which visualize the distribution of the dissimilarities to the medoids in the k frequency groups. Finally, an R^2 statistic and an F test can be calculated to assess the goodness of fit of the relative frequency sequence plot. As the quality of the results is affected by several analytical choices (sorting criterion, chosen dissimilarity measure, number of frequency groups), we recommend evaluating and comparing different solutions.

When dealing with large amounts of sequences, relative frequency sequence plots are a very powerful visualization tool ensuring readability and visual appeal by rendering a representative selection of medoids instead of all sequences, as would be the case in a regular index plot. As general heuristic, Fasang and Liao (2014) recommend dividing the sample into approximately 100 frequency groups. If colored figures are not an option, it is reasonable to reduce the number of rendered medoid sequences further, particularly if the alphabet comprises more than four states. However, this is a feasible strategy only if the resulting plot still accurately represents the data. Figure 2.6 presents such a parsimonious version of a

Figure 2.6 Relative frequency sequence plot and boxplot of dissimilarities to medoids

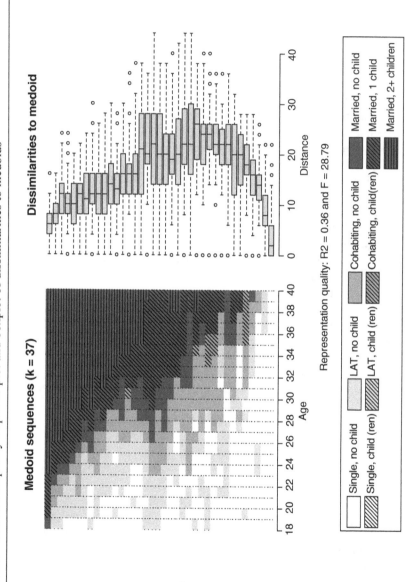

relative frequency sequence plot, which renders only 37 medoid sequences, each representing approximately 50 sequences. On the companion page, we present alternative specifications with more frequency groups that produce results very similar to those presented here.

Unlike the state distribution plots presented earlier, the relative frequency sequence plot in the left panel of Figure 2.6 provides information on the temporal order of states. The plot indicates, for instance, that the family trajectories in the pairfam sample are characterized by a close link between marriage and the transition to parenthood, which typically is observed within the first 3 years of marriage. The figure also shows that marriage usually is preceded by a cohabitation spell, which tends to be longer among those who marry later.

The box-and-whisker plot on the right panel of Figure 2.6 shows how well the 37 medoids represent their respective frequency groups. The medoids are most similar to the other sequences in their frequency group among those who marry before they turn 30 and have two or more children within these marriages, and among those who neither marry nor become parents and instead remain single most of the time. The more turbulent medoid sequences in between show higher distances to the sequences they ought to represent.

Comparing the state distribution plot (Figure 2.3) with the relative frequency sequence plot (Figure 2.6) reveals marked differences in the distribution of states at different positions of the sequences. At age 40, for instance, the proportion of unmarried persons in the distribution plot is approximately twice as high, while at age 18, the share of singles among the medoids is much higher than the corresponding proportion in the distribution plot. These differences call for caution when interpreting (the prevalence of states in) relative frequency plots. The frequency groups with higher distances to their medoid most likely comprise a notable share of sequences that are characterized by states that are not identical to the respective medoid states. As a result, the distribution of states derived from a relative frequency plot should be considered reliable only if the plot has a high goodness of fit and if it corresponds with the actual distribution in the full data. Note, however, that the observed discrepancy of the state distribution does not indicate that the relative frequency sequence plot is wrong. It merely reminds us of the fact that this plot is a technique that is reducing the complexity of sequence data by plotting only a selection of representative sequences. According to Fasang and Liao (2014, p. 658), it performs best "when there is strong but fuzzy patterning in the data, that is, when there is patterning into similar sequences but there are few identical sequences." In most applications, the degree of fuzzy patterning and thus the quality of the plot can and should be increased by plotting more homogeneous subgroups rather than the full sample. Rendering relative frequency plots of family trajectories by the level of education or gender, for instance, would produce more accurate and insightful representations of the data.

2.5 Description of Sequences II: Assessing Sequence Complexity and Quality

Except for representative sequences, the descriptive tools introduced in Section 2.3 are providing aggregated summary measures or cross-sectional snapshots of sequence data. In contrast, this section explores indicators for summarizing the longitudinal characteristics of individual sequences. The discussed indicators differ in their capabilities of accounting for the order of states (sequencing), the duration of states, and the quality of the states that constitute a sequence.

2.5.1 Unidimensional Measures

Sequencing—counting Transitions and Subsequences

Unidimensional indicators focus on describing one aspect of a sequence. The sequencing of states, for instance, could be captured by counting either the number of transitions or the number of subsequences of a given DSS sequence, with the latter being the more nuanced measure. That is because the number of transitions is not affected by the states between which the transitions occur, while the number of subsequences increases if more distinct states are involved; every additional distinct state adds one extra subsequence of length $k = 1$. The two sequences $x = (S, LAT, COH, MAR)$ and $y = (S, LAT, COH, S)$, for example, both contain four out of four possible transitions, but they differ in their number of subsequences with $\phi(x) = 16$ —the maximum for a sequence of length $k = 4$ and an equally sized alphabet—and $\phi(y) = 15$ (see Table 2.9). Given that sequence x contains every state only once, whereas S appears twice in sequence y, the subsequence indicator is performing better than the number of transitions in retaining the visual impression that x is more complex than y.

That said, the SA literature rarely reports the raw subsequence indicator because an increasing length of the examined sequences leads to a rapid inflation of the number of subsequences. For this reason, Elzinga (2010) proposed to use $\log_2 \phi(x)$ rather than a raw count of subsequences to measure the degree of sequencing.[3]

---

[3] Elzinga named this index *turbulence*. He used the same term for a second index that also accounts for the time spent in each state. In accordance with the literature, and in order to avoid confusion, we reserve the term *turbulence* exclusively for the second index.

Table 2.9 The subsequences of sequences x and y

Sequence $x = (S,LAT,COH,MAR); \phi(x)=16$				
$k = 0$	$k = 1$	$k = 2$	$k = 3$	$k = 4$
λ	S	S, LAT	S, LAT, COH	S, LAT, COH, MAR
	LAT	S, COH	S, LAT, MAR	
	COH	S, MAR	S, COH, MAR	
	MAR	LAT, COH	LAT, COH, MAR	
		LAT, MAR		
		COH, MAR		

Sequence $y = (S,LAT,COH,MAR); \phi(y)=15$				
$k = 0$	$k = 1$	$k = 2$	$k = 3$	$k = 4$
λ	S	S, LAT	S, LAT, COH	S, LAT, COH, S
	LAT	S, COH	S, LAT, S	
	COH	S, S	S, COH, S	
		LAT, COH	LAT, COH, S	
		LAT, S		
		COH, S		

Both the number of transitions and the logarithmic subsequence indicator can be normalized to have values between 0 and 1 by dividing them by their theoretical maximum. In the case of transitions, the maximum equals $k - 1$. The theoretical maximum of subsequences is obtained by counting the number of subsequences of a sequence that is constructed by repeating the elements of the alphabet until the length of the examined sequence is reached. Accordingly, the normalized subsequence measure for x equals 1, while it is $\frac{\log_2 15 - 1}{\log_2 16 - 1} = 0.97$ for sequence y. Note that 1 is subtracted from the logarithmic number of subsequences in the numerator and denominator to ensure a minimum of 0 for the normalized index. Otherwise, only an empty sequence could reach the minimum.

Duration—Longitudinal Shannon Entropy

Earlier, we introduced entropy as an aggregate measure of the dispersion of states at different positions of the sequences. However, the entropy index can also describe how the duration of the time spent in each state of the alphabet is distributed within individual sequences. The normalized longitudinal entropy is defined as

$$S = \frac{-\sum_{i=1}^{a} \pi_i \times \log(\pi_i)}{\log a}$$

with π_i depicting the relative frequency of time spent in state i and a indicating the size of the alphabet A. The maximum entropy value of a sequence is reached only if the same amount of time is spent in each state of the alphabet. In our earlier toy example, the entropy value for sequence x is identical with the two normalized sequencing indicators. The differences between the measures, however, become evident if we expand sequence x by attaching the same states once again—$x_2 = (S, LAT, COH, MAR, S, LAT, COH, MAR)$—and compare it with the sequence $y_2 = (S, S, LAT, LAT, COH, COH, MAR, MAR)$. In this example, we still obtain a Shannon entropy of 1 for both sequences, whereas only sequence x_2 reaches the maximum number of subsequences ($\phi = 224$) and transitions ($k - 1 = 7$). Sequence y_2 comprises only three transitions and 16 distinct subsequences, which translates into a normalized subsequence index of 0 and a normalized index of $\frac{\log_2 16 - 1}{\log_2 224 - 1} = 0.44$ transitions of $3/7 = 0.43$.

2.5.2 Composite Indices

In what follows, we introduce well-established measures that consider sequencing and duration simultaneously. These indices are complemented by more recent approaches that factor in a feature that is even more difficult to measure, sequence quality. Table 2.10 provides a comparison of the different indices for a set of constructed partnership sequences using the same alphabet as for our pairfam partnership sequences.

The table illustrates how the description and comparison of sequences hinge on the chosen indicator. Sequences 5 and 6, for instance, are identical in terms of sequencing. However, they obviously differ in terms of the distribution of times spent in different states (see entropy values). In contrast, the distribution of state durations is identical in sequences 11 and 12 (resulting in the same entropy of 0.68) while the sequences differ with regard to sequencing, with one additional transition observed in sequence

Table 2.10 Comparison of longitudinal sequence indices

ID	Sequence	Transitions	Entropy	Turbulence	Complexity	Precarity	Quality
1	(S,20)	0.00	0.00	0.00	0.00	0.20	0.00
2	(MAR,20)	0.00	0.00	0.00	0.00	0.00	1.00
3	(MAR,5)-(COH,5)-(LAT,5)-(S,5)	0.16	1.00	0.47	0.40	0.73	0.07
4	(S,5)-(LAT,5)-(COH,5)-(MAR,5)	0.16	1.00	0.47	0.40	0.20	0.43
5	(S,3)-(LAT,1)-(COH,6)-(MAR,10)	0.16	0.82	0.27	0.36	0.20	0.74
6	(S,4)-(LAT,4)-(COH,6)-(MAR,6)	0.16	0.99	0.42	0.39	0.20	0.50
7	(MAR,6)-(S,4)-(LAT,4)-(COH,6)	0.16	0.99	0.42	0.39	0.29	0.10
8	(S,10)-(MAR,10)	0.05	0.50	0.40	0.16	0.20	0.74
9	(S,2)-(LAT,5)-(S,3)-(COH,5)-(MAR,5)	0.21	1.00	0.42	0.46	0.42	0.43
10	(S,2)-(LAT,5)-(COH,5)-(MAR,5)-(S,3)	0.21	1.00	0.43	0.46	0.50	0.36
11	(S,2)-(MAR,10)-(COH,8)	0.11	0.68	0.24	0.27	0.35	0.36
12	(S,2)-(MAR,2)-(COH,8)-(MAR,8)	0.16	0.68	0.28	0.33	0.35	0.66

12. Often, researchers are interested in both aspects and want to consider duration and sequencing at the same time. This can be achieved by the turbulence and complexity indices.

Turbulence

The turbulence index proposed by Elzinga (2010) combines the number of subsequences with the variation in the time spent in each *episode* of the sequence, whereas the entropy index considers only the total time spent in each *state*. Turbulence is defined as

$$T(x) = \log_2\left(\phi(x)\frac{s^2_{t,max}(x)+1}{s^2_t(x)+1}\right)$$

with $s^2_t(x)$ denoting the sequence's x variance of the state durations t and

$$s^2_{t,max}(x) = \left(k(x)-1\right)\left(1-\bar{t}\right)^2$$

indicating the maximum of that variance given the total duration of the sequence, with $k(x)$ denoting the length of the DSS sequence and $\bar{t}$ the average of state durations. The obtained index can be normalized by $T(x)-1/T_{max}(x)-1$, where T_{max} is defined as the turbulence value of a sequence, which is as long as the longest sequence (STS format) in the examined set of sequences and constructed by repeating the states of the alphabet until this length is reached. In our example set, this would be a sequence that repeats the four partnership states five times. The turbulence index is increasing when either (a) the variance of the time spent in each state is decreasing or (b) the number of subsequences is increasing. As a result, sequences with the same number of subsequences—such as sequences 5 and 6—will have different turbulence values when they differ in terms of the variance of state durations.

Complexity

The complexity index is another composite measure simultaneously considering sequencing and duration. The index introduced by Gabadinho and colleagues (2010) combines the number of transitions and within-sequence entropy. It reads,

$$C(x) = \sqrt{\frac{\left(k(x)-1\right)}{\left(k_{STS}(x)-1\right)} * S(x)}$$

with $S(x)$ denoting the normalized entropy, $k(x)$ the length of the DSS sequence, and $k_{STS}(x)$ the length of the same sequence in STS notation. Sequences 3 to 7, for example, all have a DSS sequence length of 4 and an SPS length of 20. The quotient of the equation thus equals $(4-1)/(20-1) = 0.16$, which happens to be the normalized number of transitions. Combining two normalized indices, the complexity measure equals 0 for sequences without transitions and thus without variation in the state duration. The maximum of 1 can be reached only if the same amount of time is spent in each state and if the DSS sequence is of the same length as the STS sequence.

Although turbulence and complexity take different approaches to generate a composite measure, they are usually highly correlated. In our set of constructed sequences, the correlation is 0.87. In the pairfam data of yearly partnership trajectories, we obtain a correlation of 0.89. Both indicators provide information on the unpredictability or instability of sequences and are of most use if they are analyzed in tandem with other variables to compare different subgroups. While most SA applications still focus on the comparison and clustering of sequences using dissimilarity measures (Chapters 3 and 4), the analytical potential of composite indices is increasingly acknowledged in more recent applications (Biemann et al., 2011; Van Winkle, 2018; Van Winkle & Fasang, 2017). Table 2.11 illustrates one possible application using the turbulence and complexity of combined fertility and partnership sequences as a dependent variable in a simple linear regression model. The results indicate that family biographies are less predictable among highly educated persons, whereas the sequences of first-generation migrants are less complex or turbulent than those of the autochthonous majority. Further analysis revealed that the migrants' comparatively low complexity and turbulence scores are driven by their earlier onset of family formation and a high prevalence of the status "married, at least two children," which is their sequences' modal state for 12 out of 22 years (compared to 8 for the persons without a migration background). Compared to most standard dependent variables in social science applications, composite indices are rather complex outcome measures that summarize multiple aspects of sequence data, such as sequencing and duration of states. Moreover, substantively different sequences can exhibit the same degree of complexity or turbulence. As a result, single indicators, such as education or gender, tend to capture only a small share of the variation of these outcome measures, which is also the case in our example regression shown in Table 2.11.

A New Wave of Composite Measures Assessing Sequence Quality

Although they provide a good summary of sequence volatility, turbulence and complexity do not consider potential qualitative differences

Table 2.11 Composite indices used dependent variables in linear regressions

	Turbulence	Complexity
Intercept	0.29***	0.32***
	(0.00)	(0.00)
Woman (ref.: man)	−0.01**	−0.01
	(0.00)	(0.01)
Education: high school	0.04***	0.04***
	(0.00)	(0.01)
Migration status (ref.: no migration background)		
1st generation	−0.04***	−0.04***
	(0.01)	(0.01)
2nd generation	0.01	0.01
	(0.01)	(0.01)
Observations	1,809	1,809
R^2	0.06	0.05

$^*p < 0.05$; $^{**}p < 0.01$; $^{***}p < 0.001$; standard errors in parentheses.

between individual states and transitions. Sequences 3 and 4 from Table 2.10, for instance, comprise the same states but in reverse order. For each of the first four indicators displayed in the table (transitions, entropy, turbulence, and complexity), these two sequences produce identical results. Many people, however, would argue that there is a qualitative difference in family biographies of persons who see their marriage ended and those of persons who end up being married.

Against this background, several approaches have been suggested to measure sequence quality or weight existing composite indices by a factor grasping sequence quality (Brzinsky-Fay, 2007; Van Winkle & Fasang, 2017). Among the most elaborated approaches in this domain of the SA literature are the indices that have been suggested by Ritschard et al. (2018) and Manzoni and Mooi-Reci (2018). Computing these and related indices requires that the researcher specify some sort of qualitative hierarchy between the states of an alphabet. That is, some states or transitions between states, such as from unemployed to employed or from divorced to married, have to be declared as more positive or desirable than others. In most social science applications, establishing a quality hierarchy involves normative and controversial decisions that might be difficult to defend and thus should be made explicit when they are imposed.

The precarity index is based on the complexity index $C(x)$ and combines it with a notable set of other parameters that will be described only briefly here. For a more detailed introduction to the index, we refer to Ritschard et al. (2018). The index is defined as

$$prec(x) = \lambda a(x_1) + (1 - \lambda) C(x)^\alpha (1 + q(x))^\beta$$

The basic idea is to weight the well-established complexity index by a correction factor measuring whether positive or negative transitions mainly characterize a sequence. In focusing on transitions, the correction factor does not consider the time spent in high- or low-quality states. The precarity index increases with the number of negative transitions and the degree of complexity. The default correction factor is obtained by subtracting the proportion of positive transitions from the proportion of negative transitions: $q(x) = q(x)^- - q(x)^+$. The index allows for several different approaches to determine $q(x)$, which include the exclusive consideration of positive or negative transitions or the assignment of weights for different transitions. The parameter $a(x_1)$ denotes the precarity of sequence x's starting state and the parameters control the relevance of the different components of the index: λ controls the relative importance of the sequence's starting state vis-à-vis the weighted complexity index, whereas the exponents α and β specify the relevance of the complexity index as opposed to the correction factor.

Apart from those parameters, and most importantly, the researcher has to assign a rank order to the states of the alphabet, which allows distinguishing precarious from positive transitions. Initially, the index was developed to study employment trajectories, for which it is easier to establish a hierarchy between states than for family trajectories. That said, even for employment trajectories, it might not be straightforward to establish a rank order between all states of an alphabet. While it might seem reasonable to justify that being full-time employed is better than being unemployed, things become much more complicated if the alphabet also comprises states such as part-time employment or higher education. Given the common lack of clear hierarchies, the index allows the researcher to assign the same rank to multiple states (class of equivalent states) or declare them to be noncomparable states. Transitions that involve noncomparable states or that occur between equivalent states do not contribute to the correction factor.

In sum, the precarity index is a very flexible tool to jointly consider a sequence's order of states, state duration, and quality. The flexibility, however, comes at a high price: The results very much hinge on the specification of various complex parameters and thus provide an easy target for critique. The developers of the index argue that the "index provides most often sensible results with default parameter values and automatic methods for setting transition weights and starting precarity degrees" (Ritschard et al., 2018, p. 293). That said, we recommend recalculating the index with slightly adjusted parameters as a robustness check until the statistical properties of the index have been further evaluated by additional research.

Although in our view, the precarity index does not lend itself particularly well to studying partnership trajectories, we calculated it for the example sequences in Table 2.10 using the default parameters. Accordingly, we only had to specify a rank order of states. Taking a traditionalist's perspective, we came up with the following rank order of partnership states:

$$MAR > COH > LAT > S$$

Because the correction factor of the precarity index is not affected by the time spent in states of different quality, sequences with the same order of transitions end up with the same $q(x)$. If a sequence includes only positive transitions, $q(x)$ equals 0 and the precarity index boils down to the weighted precarity of the sequence's starting state. The precarity vector for the states in our alphabet is $S = 1, LAT = 0.67, COH = 0.33, MAR = 0$. With the default λ of 0.2, the precarity index for the sequences 4, 5, 6, and 8, which all include only upward transitions, therefore equals 0.2. The same is true for sequence 1 with a complexity of 0 and single as the starting state. These results illustrate that quite different sequences can have the same score on the precarity index either because they experience only positively evaluated transitions or no transitions at all. As already indicated by the term *precarity*, the index's main aim is to grasp negatively rated or precarious transitions. This becomes obvious in sequences 9 and 10, which are characterized by the same entropy but show different precarity scores. Both sequences contain one downward transition. While sequence 9 transitions from a LAT relationship into the single state, sequence 10 moves from marriage to singlehood. Given our hierarchy of states, the latter is a much more precarious transition, yielding a higher precarity score for sequence 10.[4]

The sequence quality index proposed by Manzoni and Mooi-Reci (2018) is another recent effort to go beyond the traditional composite measures.

---

[4] For a more refined application proposing a weighted partnership complexity index based on the precarity index, we refer to Hiekel and Vidal (2020).

The index is re-introducing an idea which was originally developed under the label integrative potential or capability in a research paper studying school-to-work transitions by Brzinsky-Fay (2007). Given that Manzoni and Mooi-Reci (2018) provide a more formal and general discussion of the index, we refer to it as quality index instead of using the term integrative capability that seems to be coined specifically for the study of employment trajectories. Different from the precarity index, this approach is interested in the quality of states rather than the quality of transitions. Quality is assessed by dividing the alphabet into states of success and states of failure. The resulting dichotomous sequences are evaluated to create a quality index that increases with the number of states indicating success. In addition, the index embraces the principle that more recent successes should contribute more to sequence quality than successes from the past. The index reads

$$\gamma^w\left(x^k\right) = \frac{\sum_{i=1}^{k} p_i^w}{\sum_{i=1}^{k} i^w}, \text{ with } p_i \begin{cases} i \text{ if } x_i = S \\ 0 \text{ otherwise} \end{cases}$$

where i indicates the position within the sequence, $x_i = S$ denotes a state of success at position i, and w is a weighting factor that affects how strong and fast the index reacts to and recovers from failure states.

Before we turn to the example sequences shown in Table 2.10, we illustrate the impact of different weighting factors using the following little sequence: *(S,2-LAT,1-COH,1-MAR,2)*. *MAR* is considered a success, while all other states are deemed to be failures.

$$\gamma^0 = \frac{0+0+0+0+1+1}{1+1+1+1+1+1} = 0.33; \gamma^1 = \frac{0+0+0+0+5+6}{1+2+3+4+5+6} = 0.52;$$

$$\gamma^2 = \frac{0+0+0+0+5^2+6^2}{1^2+2^2+3^2+4^2+5^2+6^2} = 0.67$$

If the weight equals 0, the quality index is just indicating the proportion of successful states. A recent success counts just as much as earlier successes. Increasing the size of the weight changes this behavior and emphasizes the more recent events. As a result, the example sequence's quality index is increasing with the size of the weighting factor.

The values for the quality index shown in Table 2.10 use a weight of $w = 1$. The first two indices depict the two extremes of the distribution consisting exclusively of either failure or success states. The differences in the quality scores of the two sequence pairs 9 and 10 or sequences 11 and 12 illustrate how the quality index emphasizes more recent states of success. In both pairs, the sequences comprise the same number of states spent in marriage. However, these states appear in different positions. As a result, the quality index is higher for sequences 9 and 11, in which the marriage spell occurs at the end of the sequences. The recency of the 5 marital states in sequence 9 even outweighs the 10 marital states occurring early in sequence 11 ($\gamma_9 = 0.43$; $\gamma_{11} = 0.36$). Reducing w would change this behavior by attenuating the recency effect.

In sum, the index provides a straightforward measure of sequence quality, which avoids the necessity of specifying a large number of parameters. The index can also be conceptualized as a time-varying variable by calculating it repeatedly, initially considering only a sequence's starting state and then incrementing it by one additional sequence position until the total length of the sequence is reached. In its current form, however, the calculation of the quality index requires boiling down the alphabet to two states indicating either success or failure. This arguably poses a problem for many social science applications that often call for incorporating a more nuanced hierarchy of success, as suggested by the precarity index.[5]

The computation of composite indices trying to grasp qualitative features of a sequence is an area of research that only recently gained momentum in the SA literature. Thus, the indices shown in this chapter should be considered only a small snapshot of an actively evolving field of research. A specific evaluation of composite indices in the context of life course research has been conducted by Pelletier et al. (2020). For a very recent, more detailed, and comprehensive review of this field, we refer to the excellent overview article by Ritschard (2021).

---

[5] On the companion page, we present a generalized version of the sequence quality index that allows the researcher to specify a quality hierarchy containing more than two states.

CHAPTER 3

COMPARING SEQUENCES

This chapter introduces techniques to compare whole sequences. In the sequence analysis (SA) framework, comparing sequences implies assessing to what extent sequences are different from one another. The first group of techniques to quantitatively assess this difference relies on optimal matching (OM) and its extensions: The degree of dissimilarity[1] between pairs of sequences is quantified by the type and number of data operations that are needed to transform one sequence into the other. As this transformation entails the alignment of the two sequences, these are also referred to as alignment algorithmic techniques. The second group of techniques compares sequences by considering how dissimilar the count of common attributes or the distribution of states and their duration are. These are, therefore, nonalignment combinatorial techniques, as sequences are not transformed in order to be compared. Both the extensions to OM and nonalignment techniques were developed to address the criticisms of classical OM as applied in the social sciences. Hence, this chapter first introduces OM and then presents alternative specifications of alignment and one selected nonalignment technique, discussing how they address some of the weaknesses of OM. We then offer a tool to compare across the dissimilarity matrices that result from the use of different dissimilarity measures. Finally, we apply what we have learned so far on computing dissimilarities between one-dimensional sequences (e.g., family biographies or individual voting behavior) to the case of multichannel sequence analysis, which allows researchers to calculate dissimilarities for multiple

---

[1] We are aware of the rich literature on the conceptual and axiomatic differences of the concepts *similarity*, *dissimilarity*, and *distance* that shows, for instance, that similarity is not the opposite of distance. We point the readers interested in an in-depth discussion to the excellent paper by Elzinga and Studer (2019). That said, we consider it beyond the scope of this book to engage in this very technical debate and, for the sake of readability, decided to (a) define a pair of sequences with a smaller dissimilarity compared to another pair of sequences as *more similar*, although it would be more appropriate to define them as *less dissimilar*; and (b) use the term *dissimilarity* when we are referring to a quantitative evaluation of the degree of mismatch between two sequences in general, and the term *distance* when referring to cases where the measure is supposed to satisfy metric axioms (see Studer & Ritschard, 2016, for a similar approach).

sets of sequences simultaneously (e.g., for employment and family trajectories or for the electoral behavior of spouses).

3.1 Dissimilarity Measures to Compare Sequences

Comparing sequences means understanding how the empirical realizations of the process they represent differ from one another. These differences are as follows (Billari et al., 2006; Settersten & Mayer, 1997; Studer & Ritschard, 2016):

- States appearing along the sequence
- Time spent in each state along the sequence
- Timing of the occurrence of each state along the sequence
- Duration of episodes within the sequences
- Sequencing of the distinct states along the sequence

As highlighted by Studer and Ritschard (2016), these aspects are intertwined. In fact, modifying the timing of the occurrence of a specific state can alter its duration and possibly the overall time spent in that state. Moreover, two sequences can be very similar with regard to one aspect (e.g., timing of the occurrence of one state) but very different with respect to another (e.g., the sequences could differ in the preceding states, which indicates a dissimilarity in sequencing).[2]

In the literature, there are two understandings of what "quantifying" dissimilarities based on timing, duration, and sequencing means. First, the degree of dissimilarity between two sequences can be assessed based on the sum of the costs of the edit operations to transform one sequence into the other—so that one is aligned to another. Procedures following this approach are known as alignment techniques or "edit distances." Alternatively, nonalignment techniques conceptualize the dissimilarity between two sequences regarding the number of common attributes that

---

[2] There are three works that can support practitioners in discriminating further between dissimilarity measures. A detailed overview of all existing dissimilarity measures can be found in Studer and Ritschard (2016), although they test the sensitivity to timing, duration, and sequencing using simulation on sequences of only binary states and therefore not directly extended to more complex cases. Halpin (2014) and Robette and Bry (2012) compare some selected measures by testing the correlation between the obtained dissimilarity matrices using real data.

sequences share or the distances between probability distributions of the states across the sequences.
Before presenting selected dissimilarity measures belonging to these two approaches, there is one final point to note. The vast majority of empirical applications utilize the pairwise dissimilarity matrix as input for further analyses (such as clustering or multidimensional scaling) that require the mathematical conditions of a metric dissimilarity to be fulfilled. Metric dissimilarities are, in fact, distances (Chen et al., 2009; Elzinga, 2007; Halpin, 2014) if, for sequences a, b, and c, (a) the distance between the two sequences is 0 if they are identical, (b) distances are always positive, (c) the distances are symmetric, and (d) the distance between sequences a and b cannot be greater than the distance between sequences a and c (or any other sequence) plus the distance between sequences c and b. Formally, for a distance $\Delta(a,b)$, metricity is given when

$$\Delta(a,b) = 0 \leftrightarrow a \text{ and } b \text{ are the same}$$

$$\Delta(a,b) \geq 0$$

$$\Delta(a,b) = \Delta(b,a)$$

$$\Delta(a,b) \leq \Delta(a,c) + \Delta(c,b)$$

The latter condition refers to the notion of triangle inequality. In the following section, we focus on metric dissimilarities. For a detailed review of these and alternative nonmetric dissimilarity measures, we refer to Studer and Ritschard (2014, 2016).

3.2 Alignment Techniques

3.2.1 Optimal Matching

Let us consider two sequences of equal length—composed of three possible states A, B, and C—over a six-time-point observational window as displayed in Table 3.1.
These sequences can be aligned to make them the same by changing the order of the states or the length of a spell. In classical OM applications, alignment can be achieved by conducting two basic operations: insertion/deletion of a state (*indel*) and substitution of a state with another one. In

Table 3.1 Example of two sequences of equal length

	x_1	x_2	x_3	x_4	x_5	x_6
Sequence 1	A	B	B	C	C	C
Sequence 2	A	B	B	B	B	B

Table 3.2 Operations to align the two sequences of equal length (Example 1)

	x_1	x_2	x_3	x_4	x_5	x_6
Sequence 1	A	B	B	**C → B**	**C → B**	**C → B**
Operation	Equal	Equal	Equal	Substitution	Substitution	Substitution
Sequence 2	A	B	B	B	B	B

Table 3.3 Operations to align the two sequences of equal length (Example 2)

	x_1	x_2	x_3	x_4	x_5	x_6	x_7	x_8	x_9
Sequence 1	A	B	B	**B**	**B**	**B**	ϵ	ϵ	ϵ
Operation	Equal	Equal	Equal	Insertion	Insertion	Insertion	Deletion	Deletion	Deletion
Sequence 2	A	B	B	B	B	B	B	B	B

theory, there are multiple ways to combine these operations. For example, state C in positions 4, 5, and 6 can be substituted with B (see Table 3.2).

Alternatively, the three Cs can be shifted to positions 7, 8, and 9, so that state B can be inserted in their place; then the alignment is completed by deleting the trailing Cs (see Table 3.3).

In the first case, we needed three substitutions to align the two sequences, while in the second case, we needed three insertions that increase the length of sequence 1, and then three deletions to shorten it and align it with sequence 2. It has to be noted that when applying operations to one sequence, we could have applied parallel operations to the other sequence: In the first case, we could have substituted B with C (B → C) in sequence 2 instead of substituting C with B (C → B) in sequence 1.

We now know how many operations we need to align the two sequences, but we do not know how dissimilar the two sequences are. To move from the number of operations to quantifying the dissimilarity, we need to assign to each operation a "cost": The sum of the costs of all operations will be regarded as the degree of dissimilarity between the two sequences. The algorithm used for calculating the costs should automatically choose the least costly (i.e., cheapest) alternative for aligning sequences. This means that it should be capable of identifying the minimum dissimilarity between a given pair of sequences (Abbott & Forrest, 1986; Abbott & Hrycak, 1990). Put differently, the algorithm has to find the optimal solution to align the sequences given a set of costs for the *indel* and substitution operations, hence the name optimal matching. The assignment of costs is a crucial step that will be discussed at length in the next section. To conclude with this first illustrative example, we assign a cost of 1 to both the *indel* and substitution operations. Consequently, the first alignment solution has a cost of 3 because each substitution costs 1 and we had to perform 3 of them. The second alignment solution has a cost of 6 because each insertion and deletion had a cost of 1 and we had to perform 6 of them. In this case, the optimal alignment solution that minimizes the cost of transforming one sequence into the other is the first one.

However, in applications with real data, identifying all possible alignment alternatives and calculating the dissimilarity based on *indel* and substitutions are computationally intensive—especially for very long sequences. Once the *indel* and substitution costs are set, OM is able to account for all of them and return the optimal solution for each pairwise comparison for all sequences in a sample. OM is based on the Needleman-Wunsch algorithm (Needleman & Wunsch, 1970). The pairwise comparison between all sequences in a sample generates a dissimilarity matrix with as many rows and columns as the total number of sequences. Note that, technically, OM can deal with sequences of unequal length because it allows for the insertion or deletion of states to achieve alignment. For the reasons highlighted in Chapter 2, in what follows we mainly refer to sequences of equal length, while in Section 3.6, we will discuss whether and how applying normalization or other sorts of transformations to the dissimilarity matrix can enable the comparison of sequences of different length.

3.2.2 Assigning Costs to the Alignment Operations

As mentioned earlier, this step is crucial in that assigning specific *indel* and substitution costs to the alignment operations affects the identification of the optimal solution. In social science applications, substitution costs can be regarded as an indicator of substantive proximity between states (Lesnard, 2014). *Indel* operations, on the other hand, shift a section of one sequence—by either inserting or deleting states—to match it with an identically coded state at a different position in another sequence. Both procedures change the structure of one of the sequences of the pairwise comparison but in different ways. *Indel* operations emphasize the importance of the occurrence and order of events along the sequence irrespective of when they occur. They shift chunks of the sequence to match the events with the same state at a different position while distorting the initial timing of the events. Substitutions emphasize the importance of similar timing rather than the sequencing of the events.

The relationship between the costs assigned to *indel* and substitution is crucial, because it determines which aspect (duration, timing, sequencing) will be emphasized when applying OM. If a higher cost is attributed to *indel* than to substitution, the algorithm will tend to favor transformations based on substitutions that preserve the timing of events. On the other hand, if a higher cost is attributed to substitution, the algorithm will tend to favor transformations that are based on *indel* and are therefore more likely to alter the timing. The costs assigned to each operation are of greatest importance when the sequences to be compared are highly dissimilar, as several transformations will be required to align them.

We illustrate different strategies to set the costs by comparing three sequences of length $k = 6$ composed of three possible states A, B, and C (see Table 3.4):

Equal Substitution and Indel Costs. When adopting this approach, the researcher assumes that there are no theoretical reasons to distinguish between the two operations (Dijkstra & Taris, 1995). Note, however, that aligning sequences of equal length by definition requires that each *indel* operation is accompanied by another one. That said, applying *indels* can

Table 3.4 Example of three sequences of equal length

	x_1	x_2	x_3	x_4	x_5	x_6
Sequence 1	A	B	B	C	C	C
Sequence 2	A	B	B	B	B	B
Sequence 3	B	C	C	C	B	B

still be cheaper than using substitutions (see Tables 3.6 and 3.7). The simplest strategy would be to assign the value of 1 to both of them: In this case, the dissimilarity between two sequences corresponds to the smallest number of operations required to align them.

Irrespective of the assigned cost parameters, the lowest alignment costs can be identified by the Levenshtein distance algorithm (Levenshtein, 1966; Sankoff & Kruskal, 1983). Table 3.5 displays the Levenshtein matrix that spells out the steps undertaken by the algorithm to identify the optimal solution when comparing sequences 1 and 2. The cells in grey identify the steps when aligning sequences and calculating costs. The first operation is the substitution between B and C in position x_4, followed by two other substitutions between B and C in positions x_5 and x_6. Each of the operations has a cost of 1 so that the dissimilarity between the two sequences is 3.

The set of operations to align each pair of sequences as well as the resulting dissimilarity matrix are summarized in Table 3.6. Sequence 1 is more similar to sequence 2 ($diss_{(1,2)} = 3$) than to sequence 3 ($diss_{(1,3)} = 4$) as fewer operations are needed for the alignment. Sequence 3 is equally similar to sequences 1 and 2, as in both cases dissimilarity is equal to 4.

The dissimilarity is metric, as the costs are symmetric, they fulfill the triangle inequality, and the distance from an object to itself is 0.

Levenshtein II Distance. An alternative approach consists of setting *indel* costs at lower than half of the minimum substitution cost so that only *indel* operations will be used. This emphasizes the similarities in terms of order rather than the timing of the events along the sequences (Lesnard, 2010). The set of operations to align sequences pairwise and the resulting dissimilarity matrix obtained by setting *indel* = 1 and substitution = 4 are displayed in Table 3.7.

In this case, sequence 1 is more similar to sequence 3 ($diss_{(1,3)} = 4$) than to sequence 2 ($diss_{(1,2)} = 6$) due to the sole use of *indel* operations, which alter the structure of the sequence and emphasize the order of events as the most important comparison criterion.

Table 3.5 Levenshtein matrix for the alignment of sequences

Note: Sequence 1 and Sequence 2 as in Table 3.4; costs: *indel* = 1 and substitution = 1.

Substitution Deletion	Insertion Σ		A		B		B		B		B		B		B	
		0	/	**1**	/	**2**	/	**3**	/	**4**	/	**5**	/	**6**	/	
A	/	/	0	1	/	1	/	1	/	1	/	1	/	1	/	
	1	**1**	**0**	**1**	**1**	**2**	**3**	**4**	**5**	**6**						
B	/	1	**0**	/	1	/	1	/	1	/	1	/	1	/		
	1	/	1	/	**1**	/	**2**	**3**	**4**	**5**						
B	/	2	1	/	1	**1**	**0**	/	1	/	1	/	1	/		
	1	/	1	/	1	/	**1**	**2**	**3**	**4**						
C	/	3	2	/	1	/	1	**1**	**0**	/	1	/	1	/		
	1	/	1	/	1	/	1	/	**1**	**2**	**3**					
C	/	4	3	/	2	/	2	/	1	**1**	/	1	/	1	/	
	1	/	1	/	1	/	1	/	1	/	**2**	**3**				
C	/	5	4	/	3	/	2	/	2	/	2	**2**	**1**	/		
	1	/	1	/	1	/	1	/	1	/	1	/	**1**	**3**		
		6	/	5	/	4	/	3	/	3	/	3	/	3		
	4	4	5	4	3	4	3	3								

Sequence 2
Sequence 1

Table 3.6 Operations to align three sequences pairwise and the resulting dissimilarity matrix

	x_1	x_2	x_3	x_4	x_5	x_6
Sequence 1	A	B	B	C	C	C
Operation	Equal	Equal	Equal	Substitution	Substitution	Substitution
Cost	0	0	0	1	1	1
Sequence 2	A	B	B	B	B	B

	x_1	x_2	x_3	x_4	x_5	x_6	x_7
Sequence 1	A	B	B	C	C	–	C
Operation	Deletion	Equal	Substitution	Equal	Equal	Insertion	Substitution
Cost	1	0	1	0	0	1	1
Sequence 3	–	B	C	C	C	B	B

	x_1	x_2	x_3	x_4	x_5	x_6
Sequence 2	A	B	B	B	B	B
Operation	Substitution	Substitution	Substitution	Substitution	Equal	Equal
Cost	1	1	1	1	0	0
Sequence 3	B	C	C	C	B	B

	Sequence 1	Sequence 2	Sequence 3
Sequence 1	0	3	4
Sequence 2	3	0	4
Sequence 3	4	4	0

Note: Sequences 1, 2, and 3 as in Table 3.4; costs: *indel* = 1 and substitution = 1.

Table 3.7 Operations to align three sequences pairwise and the resulting dissimilarity matrix

	x_1	x_2	x_3	x_4	x_5	x_6	x_7	x_8	x_9
Sequence 1	A	B	B	C	C	C	—	—	—
Operation	Equal	Equal	Equal	Deletion	Deletion	Deletion	Insertion	Insertion	Insertion
Cost	0	0	0	1	1	1	1	1	1
Sequence 2	A	B	B	—	—	—	B	B	B

	x_1	x_2	x_3	x_4	x_5	x_6	x_7	x_8
Sequence 1	A	B	B	C	C	C	—	—
Operation	Deletion	Deletion	Equal	Equal	Equal	Equal	Insertion	Insertion
Cost	1	1	0	0	0	0	1	1
Sequence 3	—	—	B	C	C	C	B	B

	x_1	x_2	x_3	x_4	x_5	x_6	x_7	x_8	x_9
Sequence 2	A	B	B	B	—	—	—	B	B
Operation	Deletion	Deletion	Deletion	Equal	Insertion	Insertion	Insertion	Equal	Equal
Cost	1	1	1	0	1	1	1	0	0
Sequence 3	—	—	—	B	C	C	C	B	B

	Sequence 1	Sequence 2	Sequence 3
Sequence 1	0	6	4
Sequence 2	6	0	6
Sequence 3	4	6	0

Note: Sequences 1, 2, and 3 as in Table 3.4; costs: *indel* = 1 and substitution = 4.

Hamming Distance. This measure stresses the timing of state occurrence. It does not allow for *indel* operations and therefore can be used only with sequences of equal length, so that the dissimilarity between two sequences is determined exclusively by the substitutions needed to align them (Hamming, 1950). The dissimilarity matrix (Table 3.8) resulting from a setting with substitution costs of 1 and no *indel* operations shows that when emphasizing the timing, sequence 1 is more similar to sequence 2 ($diss_{(1,2)} = 3$) than to sequence 3 ($diss_{(1,3)} = 5$).[3]

Considering the alignment steps, it is clear that in sequences 1 and 2, three positions are equal (A-B-B in positions x_1, x_2, and x_3), while this is the case for only one position when comparing sequences 2 and 3 (left panels in Table 3.8). Substantively, this can be interpreted as sequences 1 and 2 being more similar in terms of the timing of event occurrence.

Alternative Classical OM Specification. A fairly common strategy is to set *indel* = 1 and substitution = 2. This cost specification does not prevent by definition the use of one of the two operations (as the Hamming distance does). Substituting one state with another will cost more than inserting or deleting one position, but it might still be the best solution in some cases regarding the global optimization of matching. For our example, the dissimilarity matrix (Table 3.9) shows that sequence 1 is now more similar to sequence 3 ($diss_{(1,3)} = 4$) than to sequence 2 ($diss_{(1,2)} = 6$). In fact, as displayed in Table 3.9, the optimal alignment of sequences 1 and 2 implies three substitutions that now have a cost of 2 each, while for sequences 1 and 2 we need more operations (4 *indel*), which, however, cost less (1 each).

3.2.3 Critiques of Classical OM

OM has been criticized for the weak link between substantive theory, time, and the specification of the transformation costs (Levine, 2000).

While theories in the social sciences might provide some guidance to hierarchically order the states of the alphabet, they usually lack the level of accuracy required to clearly specify the substitution costs between all possible state combinations. In the case of employment trajectories, for instance, it is safe to say that full-time employment is less distant to part-time employment compared to being unemployed, but it is difficult to exactly quantify the differences between the states. Accordingly, most cost

---

[3] In some instances, the Hamming distance can be considered a nonalignment technique (Studer & Ritschard, 2016) because the absence of *indel* costs implies that the algorithm uses substitution only and de facto counts equal occurrences position-wise.

Table 3.8 Operations to align three sequences pairwise and the resulting dissimilarity matrix

	x_1	x_2	x_3	x_4	x_5	x_6
Sequence 1	A	B	B	C	C	C
Operation	Equal	Equal	Equal	Substitution	Substitution	Substitution
Cost	0	0	0	1	1	1
Sequence 2	A	B	B	B	B	B

	x_1	x_2	x_3	x_4	x_5	x_6
Sequence 1	A	B	B	C	C	C
Operation	Substitution	Substitution	Substitution	Equal	Substitution	Substitution
Cost	1	1	1	0	1	1
Sequence 3	B	C	C	C	B	B

	x_1	x_2	x_3	x_4	x_5	x_6
Sequence 2	A	B	B	B	C	C
Operation	Substitution	Substitution	Substitution	Substitution	Equal	Equal
Cost	1	1	1	1	0	0
Sequence 3	B	C	C	C	B	B

	Sequence 1	Sequence 2	Sequence 3
Sequence 1	0	3	5
Sequence 2	3	0	4
Sequence 3	5	4	0

Note: Sequences 1, 2, and 3 as in Table 3.4; costs: *indel* = NA and substitution = 1.

Table 3.9 Operations to align three sequences pairwise and the resulting dissimilarity matrix

	x_1	x_2	x_3	x_4	x_5	x_6
Sequence 1	A	B	B	C	C	C
Operation	Equal	Equal	Equal	Substitution	Substitution	Substitution
Cost	0	0	0	2	2	2
Sequence 2	A	B	B	B	B	B

	x_1	x_2	x_3	x_4	x_5	x_6	x_7	x_8
Sequence 1	A	B	B	C	C	C	–	–
Operation	Deletion	Deletion	Equal	Equal	Equal	Equal	Insertion	Insertion
Cost	1	1	0	0	0	0	1	1
Sequence 3	–	–	B	C	C	C	B	B

	x_1	x_2	x_3	x_4	x_5	x_6	x_7
Sequence 2	A	B	–	B	B	B	B
Operation	Deletion	Equal	Insertion	Substitution	Substitution	Equal	Equal
Cost	1	0	1	2	2	0	0
Sequence 3	B	C	C	C	B	B	B

	Sequence 1	Sequence 2	Sequence 3
Sequence 1	0	6	4
Sequence 2	6	0	6
Sequence 3	4	6	0

Note: Sequences 1, 2, and 3 as in Table 3.4; costs: *indel* = 1 and substitution = 2.

specifications suffer from a certain level of arbitrariness regarding the cost specification. Using constant substitution costs instead of theory-driven costs, however, is also problematic because this cost scheme rests on the assumption that all states are equally different from each other. Irrespective of the chosen cost specification, another criticism is that the costs are constant throughout the process, meaning that a transition from A to B at the beginning of the sequence costs the same as the same transition later on. The implications of time-invariant transformation costs become clear when thinking about, for example, the transition to parenthood in adolescence or in late adulthood. Substituting the state "childless" with the state "parent" comes at the same cost, regardless of whether the transition is observed at age 15 or 45. Finally, the transformation costs do not properly account for ordering and timing (Wu, 2000), first, because the order of the process is not respected. The substitution of A with B costs the same as the substitution of B with A. This is not problematic when comparing DNA strings, but it does not translate well into the realm of social processes; an example of this is when we substitute marriage with divorce or divorce with marriage. It is not just that these transformations have the same cost but are very different types of transitions; aligning the sequences using these transformations also alters the order of the events.

Extensions of classical OM based on alignment that manipulate substitution costs (see the next section) as well as alternative nonalignment techniques (Section 3.4) have been developed to address these criticisms.[4] In what follows, we review a selection of the most widely used options that were identified as being a good trade-off in terms of sensitivity to timing, order, duration, and computation complexity (for a compound review, see Studer & Ritschard, 2014, 2016).

3.3 Alignment-Based Extensions of OM

Theory-Based Costs. This strategy builds on prior knowledge about the process under study to define substantive costs for the transformation operations. Ideally, substitution costs should reflect the magnitude of substantive differences between states. However, because the states of a sequence alphabet are only rarely ordinal or metric, adjusting costs to reflect the "size" of the differences between states is not straightforward. In

---

[4] Additional advances in this respect are the monothetic divisive algorithms for nonrecurrent sequences (Billari & Piccarreta, 2001, 2005; Piccarreta & Billari, 2007) and a machine-learning approach to timing, sequencing, and frequency of life events (Billari et al., 2006).

many cases, it might not be feasible to justify every single cost specification based on theoretical expectations. Theory-based costs can account for impossible transitions between states by assigning the corresponding transformation a very high cost, so that the OM algorithm is unlikely to use it. This cost specification strategy can be applied to both substitution and *indel* costs.[5] In the case of our family formation trajectories, for instance, a researcher might want to emphasize the importance of the partnership status over the parental status (number of children). This could be achieved by setting the substitution costs to 1 if two states indicating a different number of children within a given partnership status are substituted, and to 2 for any substitution of different partnership statuses. Table 3.10 depicts the resulting substitution cost matrix.

We use this substitution cost matrix and *indel* costs of 1 for aligning the three family formation trajectories from our example data shown in Figure 3.1.

Table 3.10 Matrix of theory-based substitution costs for family formation trajectories

	S	Sc	LAT	LATc	COH	COHc	MAR	MARc1	MARc2+
S	0	1	2	2	2	2	2	2	2
Sc	1	0	2	2	2	2	2	2	2
LAT	2	2	0	1	2	2	2	2	2
LATc	2	2	1	0	2	2	2	2	2
COH	2	2	2	2	0	1	2	2	2
COHc	2	2	2	2	1	0	2	2	2
MAR	2	2	2	2	2	2	0	2	1
MARc1	2	2	2	2	2	2	1	0	1
MARc2+	2	2	2	2	2	2	1	1	0

[5] Strictly speaking, a theory-driven approach allows for manipulation of the definition of substitution costs only because *indels* are not allowed to vary. The researcher can only decide between accepting *indel* operations during the alignment at all (which is probably quite difficult from a theoretical point of view) or setting them extremely high so that the algorithm will not use them.

Figure 3.1 Three sequences of family formation trajectories extracted from the initial sample

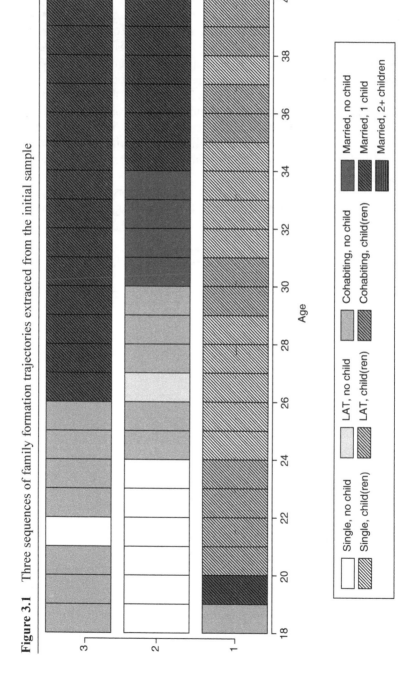

Table 3.11 Dissimilarity matrix between sequences 1, 2, and 3 from Figure 3.1 using theory-based substitution costs

	Sequence 1	Sequence 2	Sequence 3
Sequence 1	0	37	40
Sequence 2	37	0	18
Sequence 3	40	18	0

Note: Costs are *indel* = 1 and substitution = theory-based as in Table 3.10.

Optimal matching based on theory-based substitution costs returns a dissimilarity matrix between these three illustrative sequences shown in Table 3.11.

Sequences 2 and 3 are the most similar to each other ($diss_{(2,3)} = 18$). in fact, as shown in Figure 3.1, the family formation processes largely follow the same steps (single/LAT, cohabitation, marriage, and parenthood), although with a different timing. Sequences 2 and 3 are both, by contrast, highly dissimilar to sequence 1, which is composed of multiple short episodes in LAT and cohabitation across the whole observational window.

Costs Based on State Properties. In this case, the costs reflect differences in a set of properties used to distinguish between states. This strategy has the advantage of more explicitly considering the criteria according to which states are considered more or less similar to one another (Hollister, 2009). In our example on family formation trajectories, the states of the alphabet could be described by properties such as the number of children (0,1,2); existence of a partnership (yes vs. no); household structure (single vs. couple household); or civil status (single vs. married). It is possible to emphasize the importance of a feature in the calculation of the pairwise dissimilarity by assigning a higher weight to it (e.g., to the number of children). We illustrate the attributes-based dissimilarity calculation using two properties. Table 3.12 displays the values for each state of the family formation trajectories with respect to the properties "partnership status" (nominal: single or couple) and "presence of children" (binary: 0 = no, 1 = yes).[6]

---

[6] Note that one could differentiate the property "children" further by assigning ordinal values based on the actual number of children. In our case, however, some states do not distinguish between one or more children (e.g., "Single, child[ren]") and some do (e.g., "Married, 1 child" and "Married, 2 children") so that we prefer a more parsimonious specification based on presence or absence of children in each state. Consequently, the substitution costs matrix will reflect the fact that we impose no difference between "Married, 1 child" and "Married, 2 children." This is a strong assumption, which in real applications might require a substantive justification.

Table 3.12 Values for each state of the family formation trajectories with respect to the two properties "partnership status" and "presence of children"

State	Acronym	Partnership status	Presence of children
Single	S	Single	0
Single, child(ren)	Sc	Single	1
Living apart together	LAT	Couple	0
Living apart together, child(ren)	LATc	Couple	1
Cohabiting	COH	Couple	0
Cohabiting, child(ren)	COHc	Couple	1
Married	MAR	Couple	0
Married, 1 child	MARc1	Couple	1
Married, 2+ children	MARc2+	Couple	1

Having specified the values of the properties, researchers can derive pairwise substitution costs from the distances between all pairs of attribute vectors. Studer and Ritschard (2016) have suggested using the Gower dissimilarity coefficient (Gower, 1971)[7] when dealing with nominal, ordinal, and binary properties or a combination of them. Applying the Gower dissimilarity coefficient, we obtain the substitution costs matrix displayed in Table 3.13.

The substitution costs between states with the same partnership status but with and without children correspond to 0.5. The substitution costs between states that differ only in terms of the partnership status equal 0.5.

---

[7] The Gower dissimilarity coefficient (or Gower's distance) measures the similarity between two units based on the one or more variables identifying substantive characters or properties (defined as dichotomous/binary, qualitative/nominal, or quantitative/ordinal): "Two individuals i and j may be compared on a character k and assigned a score s_{ijk}, zero when i and j are considered different and a positive fraction, or unity, when they have some degree of agreement or similarity" (Gower, 1971, p. 858). As highlighted by Studer and Ritschard (2016), "Besides explicitly rendering the state comparison criteria, the approach also has the advantage of generating costs that satisfy the triangle inequality" (p. 491).

Table 3.13 Matrix of theory-based substitution costs for family formation trajectories

	S	Sc	LAT	LATc	COH	COHc	MAR	MARc1	MARc2+
S	0	0.5	0.5	1	0.5	1	0.5	1	1
Sc	0.5	0	1	0.5	1	0.5	1	0.5	0.5
LAT	0.5	1	0	0.5	0	0.5	0	0.5	0.5
LATc	1	0.5	0.5	0	0.5	0	0.5	0	0
COH	0.5	1	0	0.5	0	0.5	0	0.5	0.5
COHc	1	0.5	0.5	0	0.5	0	0.5	0	0
MAR	0.5	1	0	0.5	0	0.5	0	0.5	0.5
MARc1	1	0.5	0.5	0	0.5	0	0.5	0	0
MARc2+	1	0.5	0.5	0	0.5	0	0.5	0	0

The substitution costs between states with different values on both properties amount to 1.

If we consider the three illustrative sequences displayed in Figure 3.1, the pairwise dissimilarity matrix (Table 3.14) obtained by OM with the substitution costs shown in Table 3.13 and *indel* costs of 1 illustrates that for these cases, differences in the partnership status contribute less to the dissimilarity score than differences in the number of children. Also in this case, sequences 1 and 2 are the most dissimilar ($diss_{(1,2)} = 15.5$). While sequences 1 and 3 were the most dissimilar when using theory-based costs that clearly emphasized the relevance of the partnership status, this is not the case when using substitution costs based on state properties that account for partnership status and number of children in a more balanced fashion. In fact, sequences 1 and 2 spent more time in the same partnership states compared to sequences 1 and 3 and thus are more similar in the theory-based approach. But once partnership and parenthood status are conceptualized to contribute fairly equally to the computation of the dissimilarities, as in our definition of the costs based on state properties, sequence 1 is more similar to sequence 3.

Data-Driven Costs. This strategy relies on computing substitution or *indel* costs based on data characteristics, namely, the frequency of specific states or transitions between states. For example, higher costs can be attributed to

Table 3.14 Dissimilarity matrix between sequences 1, 2, and 3 from Figure 3.1 using state-attributes-based substitution costs

	Sequence 1	Sequence 2	Sequence 3
Sequence 1	0	15.5	9.0
Sequence 2	15.5	0	6.5
Sequence 3	9.0	6.5	0

Note: Costs are *indel* = 1 and substitution = state attributes as in Table 3.13.

transitions to/from states that occur rarely along the sequences (Piccarreta & Billari, 2007; Stovel, 2001). Studer and Ritschard (2016) suggest that the "rarity" of a state can be derived from the data using a monotonic function (logarithm or square root) of the inverse of (a) its overall observed frequency, or (b) the mean time spent in it. Alternatively, substitution costs have been derived from the reciprocal of the frequency of the transition between two states. This approach relies on the idea that states are similar if we observe frequent transitions between them (e.g., Stovel et al., 1996); note, however, that the assertion that the frequency of transitions between states is indicating substantive closeness between them often lacks a sound theoretical justification (Halpin, 2010; Lesnard, 2014).[8] Applying this approach to our three example sequences with the states A, B, and C in Table 3.4 yields the substitution cost matrix shown in Table 3.15.

An optimal matching analysis with this matrix and an *indel* cost of 1 results in the dissimilarity matrix depicted in Table 3.16.

As a matter of fact, using transitions between states to set substitution costs raises the issue of circularity, because transitions are generally calculated from sequences that are then analyzed with OM. Moreover, the output

---

[8] Two additional transition-based cost assignment strategies have been discussed in the literature. The first consists of using odds ratios of transition probabilities between all pairs of states instead of probabilities (Cornwell, 2015, p. 123). The second approach relies on time-varying transition rates, which implies that a distinct substitution cost matrix is computed for each time unit. For example, the matrix for time t is computed by considering only the states at time t and $t + 1$ instead of being based on the total number of transitions between states in the whole sequences (Gabadinho, Ritschard, Studer, & Müller, 2011); see the discussion that follows on dynamic Hamming distance.

Table 3.15   Matrix of substitution costs based on reciprocal of the frequency of the transition between states

	A	B	C
A	0	1	2
B	1	0	1.55
C	2	1.55	0

is often not metric as the resulting substitution cost matrices tend to violate the triangle inequality.

Dynamic Hamming Distance. This extension of the Hamming distance allows for varying substitution costs depending on the position of the potential substitution along the sequence. This distance measure aims at overcoming a critique regarding the decision to assign the same cost to the same operation irrespective of when it is performed along the sequence; the criticism here is that such a procedure ignores the nature of the relationship between two states at different time points along the process. For example, in the family formation process, substituting the state "single" with the state "marriage" at age 18 or 40 has a different substantive meaning based on societal expectations or the implications for the next steps of family formation. Computation-wise, the substitution costs are based on the transition rates between two states between $t - 1$ and t and between t and $t + 1$ (Lesnard, 2010). As a result, lower substitution costs for transitions between states signify that these states are more likely to co-occur in different trajectories; for example, if the transition from "single" to "married" is more frequent than the transition from "single" to "married, 1 child," the former will be less costly than the latter. However, substitution costs are not sensitive to the direction of a transition. Therefore, transition-based substitution costs are only useful when there is either a theoretical justification for the assumption that the costs are the same, independent of the direction of the transformation, or when one of the directions is impossible. (Dlouhy & Biemann, 2015, p. 170)

The dynamic Hamming distance is calculated by summing up the costs of the alignment of the two sequences at each time point. Similar to other

Table 3.16 Operations to align three sequences pairwise and the resulting dissimilarity matrix

	x_1	x_2	x_3	x_4	x_5	x_6
Sequence 1	A	B	B	C	C	C
Operation	Equal	Equal	Equal	Substitution	Substitution	Substitution
Cost	0	0	0	1.55	1.55	1.55
Sequence 2	A	B	B	B	B	B

	x_1	x_2	x_3	x_4	x_5	x_6	x_7	x_8
Sequence 1	A	B	B	C	C	C	–	–
Operation	Deletion	Deletion	Equal	Equal	Equal	Equal	Insertion	Insertion
Cost	1	1	0	0	0	0	1	1
Sequence 3	–	–	B	C	C	C	B	B

	x_1	x_2	x_3	x_4	x_5	x_6	x_7
Sequence 2	A	B	–	B	B	B	B
Operation	Deletion	Equal	Insertion	Substitution	Substitution	Equal	Equal
Cost	1	0	1	1.55	1.55	0	0
Sequence 3	–	B	C	C	C	B	B

	Sequence 1	Sequence 2	Sequence 3
Sequence 1	0	4.65	4
Sequence 2	4.65	0	5.1
Sequence 3	4	5.1	0

Note: Sequences 1, 2, and 3 as in Table 3.4; costs: *indel* = 1 and substitution = transition rates reciprocal of the frequency of the transition between states as in Table 3.15.

Table 3.17 Dissimilarity matrix between sequences 1, 2, and 3 from
Table 3.4 using substitution costs based on dynamic
Hamming distance

	Sequence 1	Sequence 2	Sequence 3
Sequence 1	0	10.5	16.0
Sequence 2	10.5	0	11.5
Sequence 3	16.0	11.5	0

Note: Costs are *indel* = 1 and substitution = dynamic Hamming distance.

data-driven cost assignment strategies based on transition rates between
states, no *indel* transformations are used, so that the measure is extremely
sensitive to timing. For our example sequences displayed in Table 3.4, the
dissimilarity matrix corresponds to that shown in Table 3.17.

3.4 Nonalignment Techniques

These metrics are based on the identification of subsequences that occur
in the same order along the sequence. Subsequences are elements that can
be extracted from the entire sequences considered; these elements are
defined as tokens and can be either the single states of the alphabet or a
combination of subsequent states that occur next to each other along the
sequences.[9] We illustrate the nonalignment techniques with just the longest common subsequence metric, but there are alternatives (e.g., the number of matching subsequences by Elzinga, 2003, or its generalized
version subsequence vector representation-based metric by Elzinga &
Studer, 2015).

Longest Common Subsequence. According to this criterion, the dissimilarity between two sequences corresponds to the length of their longest common subsequence (LCS; Elzinga, 2014); this metric counts properties

---

[9]Nonalignment techniques also include techniques based on the computation of dissimilarities between state distributions. These techniques compare sequences with respect to the
time spent in each state. The dissimilarity between sequences is measured by the distance
between the vectors of time spent in each state using either the Euclidean distance or the χ^2
distance. For details about these less commonly used dissimilarity measures, see Studer and
Ritschard (2014, 2016).

shared by two sequences. Dissimilarity based on LCS is not Euclidean because two sequences' common subsequences might occur at different positions in each of the two sequences. Therefore, this measure is not overly sensitive to timing. The LCS algorithm first identifies the number of matching elements among the compared sequences. The dissimilarity corresponds to the following:

$$diss_{LCS} = A(seq1,\ seq1) + A(seq2,\ seq2) - 2A(seq1, seq2)$$

Therefore, comparing sequences 1 and 2 from Table 3.6 amounts to

$A(seq1, seq1) = seq1$'s longest subsequence $ABBCCC = 6$

$A(seq2, seq2) = seq2$'s longest subsequence $ABBBBB = 6$

$A(seq1, seq2) = $ longest shared subsequence $ABB = 3$

$$diss_{LCS} = 6 + 6 - 2 \times 3 = 12 - 6 = 6$$

Table 3.18 reports the full pairwise dissimilarity matrix for the three sequences from Table 3.4.

As it is based on shared attributes that appear in the same order along the two sequences, this metric emphasizes dissimilarities in the sequencing and in the time spent in each state. Applying LCS generates the same results as applying OM with a substitution cost of 2 and an *indel* cost of 1.

3.5 Comparing Dissimilarity Matrices

The question of which dissimilarity measure should be chosen does not have a unique answer as it depends on the empirical question the researcher is addressing. As mentioned at the beginning of this chapter, the aspects that characterize the sequences (the states appearing, the time spent in each state, the timing and the duration of each episode) are intertwined, and although some of the dissimilarity measures reviewed earlier put more emphasis on one or more of these aspects, they might still account for the others. Moreover, most of the time we are interested in the overall temporal unfolding of the process, which means that we want to account for all of the sequence characteristics at the same time. It is good practice to be clear about the objective when comparing the sequences and to test different

Table 3.18   Dissimilarity matrix between sequences 1, 2, and 3 from
Table 3.4 using the LCS metric

	Sequence 1	Sequence 2	Sequence 3
Sequence 1	0	6	4
Sequence 2	6	0	6
Sequence 3	4	6	0

specifications. In other words, it is important to anchor choices regarding the states considered and the dissimilarity measure theoretically, as the final results will depend on these (data-driven) decisions. In fact, in most cases, the choice regarding the states is more decisive than the one on the dissimilarity measure as it directly concerns the features of the process to be analyzed.

Technically, calculating the correlation between dissimilarity matrices resulting from alternative options is useful for evaluating the degree to which different strategies return similar results. The Mantel correlation has been used for this purpose (Halpin, 2014; Piccarreta 2015; Robette & Bry, 2012). Using our full example data on family trajectories, Figure 3.2 shows the Mantel correlation coefficients for the dissimilarity matrices based on five different cost specifications: OM with *indel* = 1 and substitution = 2, OM with *indel* = 2 and substitution = 1, OM with *indel* = 1 and property-based substitution, OM with *indel* = 1 and theory-based substitution, and LCS. The coefficients are rendered in shades of gray according to the strength of the correlation. However, the strength of the pairwise correlations varies substantially, indicating factual differences in the dissimilarity measures' sensitivity to specific sequence aspects. For example, the OM with theory-based substitution costs returns results very similar to OM with *indel* = 1 and substitution = 2, whereas it correlates only moderately with the distances derived from the property-based substitution cost matrix.

In addition to inspecting the correlations, a direct comparison of the dissimilarity distributions (obtained by different approaches) might provide further insights into the commonalities and idiosyncrasies of the different measures. For this purpose, we recommend normalizing the dissimilarity matrices to ease the comparison. Note, however, that the

Figure 3.2   Mantel correlation coefficients for sequences for family
formation trajectories

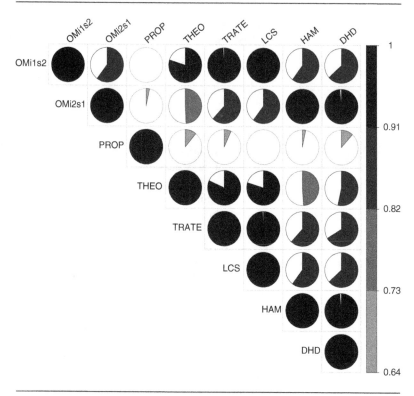

Note: OMi1s2: optimal matching with *indel* = 1 and substitution = 2; OMi2s1: optimal matching with *indel* = 2 and substitution = 1; PROP: optimal matching with *indel* = 1 and substitution = property-based costs; THEO: optimal matching with *indel* = 1 and substitution = theoretical costs; TRATE: optimal matching with *indel* = 1 and substitution = costs based on transition rates; LCS: longest common subsequence; HAM: optimal matching with *indel* = 1 and substitution = costs based on Hamming distance; DHD: optimal matching with *indel* = 1 and substitution = costs based on dynamic Hamming distance. Normalized dissimilarities.

normalizing strategy depends on the dissimilarity measure used (see Elzinga, 2014; Elzinga & Studer, 2019; Gabadinho, Ritschard, Müller, & Studer, 2011).[10]

---

[10] Note that computation of normalized distance matrices is implemented in the current version of TraMineR.

Transition Sequence Analysis

The fact that substitution costs need to be symmetrical and that substitutions between any state can be used at any point in time along the sequence during the alignment procedure raises some substantive concerns (Levine, 2000; Wu, 2000). In reality, states are not independent from whatever precedes them and some states, once visited, constitute "points of no return." For example, consider employment trajectories composed of months spent in the "1st employment episode," "2nd employment episode," and "3rd+ employment episode." Once participants have entered the second episode, it is no longer possible to go back to the first episode. The substitution costs, however, are defined anyway. Similarly, in employment trajectories distinguishing between the states "employment" and "unemployment," substituting employment with unemployment has the same cost as substituting unemployment with employment. However, these two processes have a different substantive meaning. Biemann (2011) addresses this concern by introducing an alternative strategy for specifying the alphabet based on transitions between states. Instead of coding distinct states (for instance, "employment" or "unemployment"), he is considering the current state and the state at the next time point. These newly defined states either indicate transitions between different states ("employment → unemployment" or "unemployment → employment") or state permanence ("employment → employment," "unemployment → unemployment"). The costs for substituting specific transitions with others will account for the direction (and therefore the quality) of the substitution. Importantly, the transition space might become quite large depending on the initial number of states as all combinations in both directions have to be considered.

3.6 Comparing Sequences of Different Length

As discussed in Chapter 2, there are different reasons for ending up with sequences of unequal length. First, missing time points can appear along the sequence. This is common for longitudinal data collected prospectively when individuals do not answer in a specific year and then re-enter the sample. In this case, one may consider imputing missing values (Halpin, 2016b). The second process that can lead to sequences of different length is permanent dropout from the sample, also known as sample attrition. Third, individuals (or cases in general) might simply not be "old enough"; considering the family formation process between the ages of 18 and 40, if some individuals in the sample are younger than 40 at the time of the interview, their life course will be represented by a shorter sequence that ends in correspondence to their current age. These last two cases can be considered types of "right" censoring. Fourth, sequences can be of different length when cases entered the sample at different points in time and retrospective data on their past trajectories are not collected. Finally, the different length can mirror the actual differences in length of certain processes. For example, the same production process in two factories can consist of a different number of steps, so that the sequences representing the process will have different lengths (see Stovel et al., 1996, for an application). In this latter case, the researcher wants to account exactly for such a discrepancy by calculating the differences between the processes. Accordingly, inserting or deleting elements will contribute significantly to the computation of dissimilarity. With respect to the previous instances, some sort of manipulation of the dissimilarity measures or transformation of the dissimilarity matrix may be a viable strategy to prevent sequences of unequal length from unduly affecting the calculation of the pairwise dissimilarities. Stovel and Bolan (2004) suggested using variable *indel* costs that are set lower when aligning sequences of different length compared to when aligning sequences of equal length.

Applying normalization to discount the dissimilarity between sequences in proportion to their differences in length has been suggested as an alternative approach (Gabadinho, Ritschard, Müller, & Studer, 2011; Levy et al., 2006). This is not a feasible strategy, however, because the normalization does not account for the different length of two sequences, only for the varying number of characteristics of the sequences (see Elzinga & Studer, 2019). How much sequence length should contribute to the distance between sequences and whether to impute missing or shorten longer sequences in order to work on sequences of equal length are decisions that must be justified theoretically and substantively.

3.7 Beyond the Full-Sample Pairwise Comparison

So far, we have considered pairwise comparisons between all sequences in our sample. However, the theoretical implication and substantive meaning of "dissimilarity" in this case might be ambiguous because every sequence is compared to every other sequence (Levine, 2000). Depending on the research question, alternative strategies that use substantively meaningful reference sequences as a starting point for the computation dissimilarities might be suitable.

First, based on theoretical expectations of what a specific process should look like, we might want to consider different possible empirical realizations: For example, how does the expected and actual implementation of a series of policies compare across different regions? To this purpose, one may define a reference sequence that reflects theoretical expectations about the appearance of specific states and their timing. The dissimilarity measure will be computed by comparing every sequence in the sample to the reference sequence. In the case of family trajectories, we might be interested in calculating how dissimilar individuals' realizations are from a theoretical sequence representing a traditional family formation sequence where the individual moves from single without children *(S,5)*, to married without children *(MAR,2)*, to married with one child *(MARc1,3)*, and finally married with two children *(MARc2+,12)* (see Panel a in Figure 3.3).

By setting the *indel* costs at 1 and the substitution costs at 2, we expect that the algorithm will tend to favor transformations that are based on *indel* and are therefore more likely to alter the timing, so that smaller pairwise dissimilarity values will be obtained for sequences that are more similar in the sequencing of the events rather than the timing. This is indeed the case, as the reference traditional family formation sequence has dissimilarities equal to 42, 24, and 36 to the three sequences displayed in Panel d in Figure 3.3, respectively. Sequence 2 is most similar to the traditional family formation sequence, displaying similar sequencing of the same states but with different timing. In contrast, sequence 1 is the most different because it comprises only one observation spent in a state that is also part of the reference sequence (i.e., "Married, 1 child"). Sequence 3 is slightly less dissimilar to the reference, because in three instances both sequences are observed with the same state at the same position.

Second, we might want to compare all sequences in the sample to the empirically most frequent one (Panel b in Figure 3.3). When sequences in the sample are highly heterogeneous (which might be the case when analyzing lengthy sequences with a large alphabet), the most frequent one might actually represent a very small number of sequences. For our sample, the most frequent sequence for family trajectories (S, 22) represents a mere 0.75% of the full sample (Figure 3.3). Nevertheless, this should not be a matter of concern if there are substantive reasons for making the most frequent sequence the reference. In our case, the most frequent sequence has dissimilarities equal to 44, 32, and 42 to the three displayed in Panel d in Figure 3.3, respectively.

Alternatively, one could apply another empirical strategy by choosing a representative sequence as reference. While different strategies can be applied to extract representative sequences (see Gabadinho, Ritschard, Studer, & Müller, 2011, for an overview), we focus here on the most widely used candidate by extracting the medoid sequence.

Figure 3.3 Options for comparison between each sequence in the sample and a reference sequence

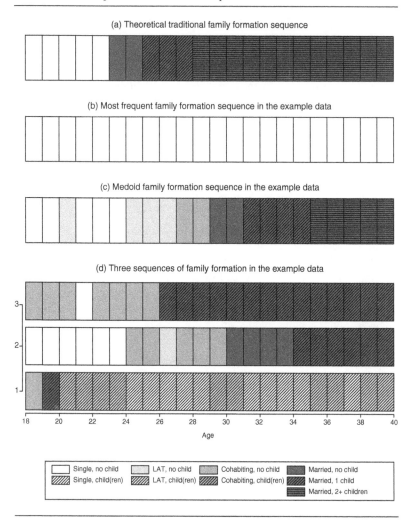

Note: The three sequences in Panel d are the same as in Figure 3.1.

The medoid is identified as the center of a pairwise dissimilarity matrix and then used as reference to calculate dissimilarities with all sequences in the sample. In our example, the medoid corresponds to the sequence *(S,2)-(LAT,1)-(S,3)-(LAT,3)-(COH,2)-(MAR,2)-(MARc1,4)-(MARc2+,5)* displayed in Panel c in Figure 3.3. Also in this case, using *indel* = 1 and substitution costs = 2, sequence 2 is most similar to the reference sequence ($diss_{(medoid,2)} = 16$, $diss_{(medoid,1)} = 40$, $diss_{(medoid,3)} = 30$), which in this case is the medoid.

Alternatively, instead of using one reference sequence for the entire sample, one could define group-specific (e.g., the medoid sequences for men and women) or even unit-specific reference sequences. The latter strategy has been increasingly applied in more recent applications: Soller (2014), for instance, examined how idealized relationship sequences of adolescents compare to their actual relationship experience observed some time later.

Finally, a recent development is the analysis of dyadic data with sequence analysis, which opened new possibilities for the interpretation of sequence dissimilarities (Liefbroer & Elzinga, 2012). Dyadic approaches lend themselves particularly well to study sequences of family members. Accordingly, dyadic applications of SA have been published mainly in this area, for instance, to explore similarities in the life courses of parents and their children or among siblings (Fasang & Raab, 2014; Karhula et al., 2019; Liefbroer & Elzinga, 2012; Raab et al., 2014).[11]

Before concluding, a reminder is necessary: When comparing all sequences to the same reference sequence, two (or more) qualitatively different sequences may have identical dissimilarity to the reference sequence. Therefore, similar to the standard full-sample pairwise comparison, we know how dissimilar sequences are (to the reference sequence), but we do not know how qualitatively different they are.[12] Also in this case, visualization and the use of summary indicators as presented in the previous chapter are key to gaining a better understanding of the qualitative differences.

---

[11] See Liao (2021) for two new measures of the similarity of dyadic sequences.

[12] As will be discussed in the next chapter, the cluster analysis requires a dissimilarity matrix as input. When computing the dissimilarity between one reference sequence and all sequences in the data set, we obtain a vector (rather than a matrix) of dissimilarities. Clustering based on this vector will identify groups where sequences have lower or higher dissimilarities from the reference sequence, rather than groups where sequences are similar to each other and dissimilar to those in other groups. Therefore, one should be careful and consider these options in light of the research question.

Accounting for the Nested Structure of Temporal Processes

Researchers in the subfield of time use studies have proposed a two-stage optimal matching to account for the fact that a temporal process is nested in a higher level process. They have also noted that because of this data structure, these processes affect each other's unfolding. For example, in order to be able to compare the structure of two workdays (lower level), it is necessary to correctly locate them within the entire week's structure (higher level). In the first stage of the two-stage optimal matching procedure introduced by Lesnard and Kan (2011), for instance, optimal matching is used to calculate dissimilarities between days for each case in the sample and to generate a typology of days; in the second stage, optimal matching is used again to make comparisons across 7-day weeks. Each day is represented by the cluster to which it was assigned in the previous step (for a similar analytical strategy, see Hepburn, 2018, 2020; for a discussion and a comparison to alternative approaches, see Minnen et al., 2016). Other strategies drawing on the idea that temporal processes can be divided into phases or intervals have been introduced in recent years, such as Collas's (2018) multiphase optimal matching, which applies optimal matching multiple times to subsequences representing substantively meaningful phases along a process. Each phase can be characterized by different alphabets of states. The matrix of pairwise dissimilarities between the full sequences is obtained by summing up the phase-specific pairwise dissimilarity matrices. Although multistage OM procedures, like the ones presented in this box, have been applied only rarely, they represent interesting and promising extensions of existing procedures for analyzing longitudinal categorical data.

CHAPTER 4

IDENTIFYING GROUPS IN DATA: ANALYSES BASED ON DISSIMILARITIES BETWEEN SEQUENCES

This chapter focuses on cluster analysis of sequence data. Cluster analysis is a set of multivariable analysis techniques that aims at partitioning data by grouping objects (in our case, sequences) in such a way that objects within a group are more similar to each other than to objects allocated to other groups. In the context of sequence analysis (SA), sequences belonging to the same cluster should display some sequential regularities, such as a similar succession of states or a similar duration of episodes. The chapter covers two widely used hard clustering algorithms in SA (Ward's linkage and partitioning around medoids) and introduces statistical and visual criteria to compare different cluster solutions. We then elaborate on how to improve construct validity for both sequence and cluster analysis by introducing heuristics that fully utilize the descriptive potential of these analytical techniques. We conclude with examples of a structural analysis of patterns. The typology identified by the cluster analysis is used as either a categorical independent or a categorical dependent variable in a multivariable regression analysis.

4.1 Clustering Sequences to Uncover Typologies

Cluster analysis is the most commonly used way to identify groups that represent empirical realizations of a given temporal social process within sequence data.[1] Because temporal social processes give rise to regularities

---

[1] Different frameworks for data reduction exist. Here, we limit the attention to a specific application of finite mixture models commonly labeled as "cluster analysis," which is the most widely used in the SA literature published so far. As discussed in this chapter, we focus on heuristic clustering algorithms, either hierarchical or partitional, that aim to group similar objects into clusters. Clusters can then be related to a set of baseline covariates or used as independent variables for outcomes eventually measured at the end of the observational window. The family of finite mixture models (see Bouveyron et al. 2019 for a review) also includes model-based clustering methods. Murphy and colleagues (2021) recently introduced such a technique to study sequences by using mixtures of

across units, data can be simplified to identify a typology where types are representative of a set of sequences containing the same regularities, that is, displaying similar patterns. Each sequence is "assigned" to a distinct type in the typology based on its similarity with the other cases in that group and the dissimilarity to cases in other groups. This procedure is known as hard or crisp clustering as opposed to fuzzy or soft clustering, where sequences are assigned a set of probabilities of belonging to each cluster (see the box on fuzzy clustering later in this chapter).

The groups emerging from the clustering procedure summarize the core features of sequences in the group, and the overall aim is to identify regularities without prior assumptions on the data-generating process that leads to specific types (Abbott, 1992; Billari, 2005). These core features can be understood as latent dimensions to be uncovered via cluster analysis. In a sense, the types substitute for the individual sequences, which are univocally assigned to a cluster.

Grouping sequences into types that represent patterns of a social process is a genuinely explorative tool. Considering the illustrative data used in the previous chapters on the family formation process, we may simply be interested in identifying a typology that describes how this very process is empirically realized in the population. Some individuals will remain single, others will enter into cohabitation and have children out of wedlock early in the life course, and others will marry at a later age after multiple LAT relationships and not have children.

However, this "explorative" approach could also represent the first step in a structural analysis of patterns. A researcher may be interested in whether such patterns emerge as a result of historical circumstances, or whether and why men and women have different likelihoods of following

---

exponential-distance models that estimate the relationship between the covariates and the clusters and simultaneously the clustering itself. A complementary framework (Kruskal, 1977; Kruskal & Wish, 1978) is represented by multidimensional scaling (MDS) that aims at obtaining geometric representations of observations in a low-dimensional (generally 2-dimensional) space. The positions are based on a certain measure of similarity or dissimilarity between the objects. In the SA literature, MDS has been used for clustering in a few applications (see Piccarreta, 2012; Piccarreta & Lior, 2010; Robette et al., 2015), but the interpretation of MDS scores tends to be less convenient and insightful than the interpretation of typologies obtained by using cluster analysis. This is particularly true when clusters or MDS scores are analyzed as dependent or independent variables in a regression framework. MDS, however, has been fruitfully combined with cluster analysis to visualize clustering results (e.g., Akkucuk, 2011) and sort sequences within clusters (e.g., Fasang & Liao, 2014).

a specific pattern, or what the consequences are of having followed a given trajectory. These questions refer to what is defined as an "institutional" approach (Bernardi et al., 2019; Levy et al., 2006) that regards typologies as the outcome of the (social) structure on trajectories (Studer, 2021): Accordingly, the regularities identified on the basis of the pairwise comparisons via dissimilarity measures are shaped by the extent to which structural factors limit the possible empirical realizations (trajectories) of a given temporal process. Actors (individuals, institutions, etc.) can be more or less aware of such structural constraints, and their agency in governing how temporal processes unfold can vary. Let us consider three cases exemplifying different degrees of pathway institutionalization: educational trajectories, the transition to adulthood, and the chronology of care needs among elderly people. In the case of educational trajectories, the steps are highly institutionalized, and individuals can only choose when to exit education after compulsory schooling and what track to follow during high school and eventually at university. In the second case, the timing of different steps throughout the transition to adulthood (finishing education, entering the labor market, starting a family) are defined by social norms and learned via socialization, but both the timing and the order of such transitions are essentially left to the individual. In these two cases, actors are aware of the typical patterns and can even use them as reference points when deciding how to act during the process, as they can anticipate what the next steps should/will be. Finally, the evolution of care needs among the elderly over time is not institutionalized in the sense of the previous two examples; there are no laws governing the process and no social norms indicating a preferred care need trajectory.

In most of the cases, researchers are interested in uncovering typologies (the descriptive approach) and in connecting types to explanatory variables or using them as explanatory variables (the institutional approach). In both cases, it is important to keep in mind that cluster analysis is a data-driven descriptive tool that simplifies complex data. The evaluation of typologies can be based on statistical and/or substantive validity (Piccarreta & Studer, 2018). Statistical validity refers to the ability to extract the "true" patterns in the data, while substantive validity refers to the identification of groups that are meaningful with respect to the research questions and the expectations based on theory. In the following sections, after introducing the rationale for cluster analysis as applied in the sequence analysis literature, we walk the reader through all the analytical steps and provide different analytical options to be explored for each step. We also discuss heuristics for choosing between the different options; that is, we will discuss how to "construct" validity.

4.1.1 The Rationale Behind Clustering Sequences

Grouping sequences using cluster analysis relies on the assumption that a sequence that represents the individual empirical realization of a temporal process shares some characteristics with other individual realizations of the same process and that these can therefore be grouped together. In other words, cluster analysis reveals the structure of the data by identifying similar patterns. Sequences grouped together should be as similar to each other as possible and as dissimilar to sequences in other groups as possible. Therefore, clustering sequences is a way to simplify complex data with the aim of producing meaningful typologies. This is achieved by ignoring minor differences between the sequences allocated to each cluster (type) and ensuring that major differences are not ignored. The aim here is to avoid drawing inaccurate conclusions, which would occur, for example, when high within-cluster heterogeneity is ignored. We will discuss more specifically what inaccurate conclusions in cluster analysis using sequences mean when discussing the issue of validation. For now, let us consider the two concepts, namely, between-cluster separation and within-cluster homogeneity, which can be analytically distinguished but are highly interrelated (high between-cluster separation is correlated with high within-cluster homogeneity) and have to be taken into account simultaneously (Studer, 2021). The plots in the first row in Figure 4.1 display three illustrative data configurations. Each set of cases (dots) is displayed on a bidimensional space depending on their pairwise dissimilarity. The cases are allocated to two groups, which are depicted using white and grey circles and separated by the vertical line within each plot. In the first configuration, the initial set of cases is characterized by low separation, as the cases allocated to the two groups are relatively similar; this is indicated by the fact that many of them lie next to the border of the cluster and very close to those in the other cluster. As we move to the top-center and top-right panels, the degree of separation increases, as cases in one cluster are increasingly further away from those in the other cluster and the two groups are, on average, increasingly dissimilar. The higher the degree of separation between the clusters, the stronger our conclusions about the structure of the data; in other words, a high degree of separation strengthens our confidence that the identified typology is appropriate because a high separation implies high differentiation between clusters.

The second key concept is within-cluster homogeneity—that is, the extent to which sequences are close to the center of the cluster. By extension, within-cluster homogeneity refers to the idea that sequences in each cluster can be summarized by referring to a single type represented by the cluster. The plots in the second row of Figure 4.1 display three illustrative

87

Figure 4.1 Illustrative example of between-cluster separation and within-cluster homogeneity

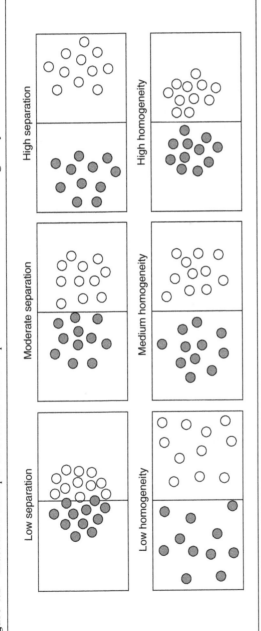

Note: Adapted from Studer (2021).

data configurations with different degrees of within-cluster homogeneity. As we move from low to medium and then to high homogeneity, the dots representing sequences get progressively closer to each other, that is, their pairwise dissimilarity becomes smaller, and, conversely, the within-cluster homogeneity increases.

High separation and high within-cluster homogeneity are pivotal when considering the association between clusters and covariates in a descriptive fashion. They are also crucial when clusters are used as predictors or outcomes in a regression framework as single cases will be replaced by the types they have been assigned to. In the case of between-cluster separation, if several sequences are positioned very close to a type other than the one they have been assigned to, this might alter the estimated relationship between the clusters and the covariates of interest. With respect to within-cluster homogeneity, low values might imply that cases within that cluster have very different values on the covariates of interests, so that it is difficult to identify any significant cluster–covariate relationship. There is not an absolute threshold for high or low separation or within-cluster homogeneity, but we can say that the lower the separation and homogeneity, the more difficult it is to identify an optimal solution. This means that the empirical work consists of testing heuristics to find quasi-optimal solutions. Likewise, in this case, the assessment is case-specific. The criteria presented in this chapter will support researchers in making decisions on the number of clusters.

4.1.2 Crisp (or Hard) Clustering Algorithms

The crisp clustering methods used in SA are based on dissimilarity values obtained by the pairwise comparison of sequences. These values condense complex sequence data by simultaneously considering multiple characteristics of the sequences, such as the timing and ordering of states (see Chapter 3). Due to this inherently simultaneous consideration of multiple features, in the context of an SA, clustering can be conceived of as a polythetic procedure.[2] Two

---

[2] Property-based and model-based clustering are exceptions in this respect, as they are referred to as monothetic divisive clustering methods based on the explicit identification of sequence features or properties (e.g., the time in each state and the age at which a specific state is experienced, the recurrence of a state, or the overall complexity, etc.). These features are then used one by one to progressively split the initial pool of sequences into clusters depending on the amount of variation explained by a given feature. For a detailed presentation of these alternatives, see Chavent et al., 2007; Piccarreta & Billari, 2007; Studer, 2018.

main families of clustering methods are used in SA, namely, hierarchical and partitional methods.[3]

Hierarchical Clustering

This family of clustering methods produces a nested set of clusters. It is left to the researcher to decide what level of the hierarchy should be considered appropriate for answering the research question. There are two approaches: divisive and agglomerative. Divisive (or top-down) approaches iteratively split the initial pool of cases into smaller and smaller clusters. This is the least common strategy, and we therefore focus on agglomerative (bottom-up) approaches, which iteratively group cases into larger and larger clusters depending on their proximity. The agglomeration is based on a linkage criterion, which is in turn based on a specific definition of proximity between clusters. Various linkage criteria can be considered, depending on what the researcher is concerned with—the proximity of one or all cases across clusters (single or complete linkage), the average proximity between cases in two clusters (average linkage), the weighted proximity for the size of the cluster (weighted average linkage), or the proximity of the most central cases of two clusters (centroid linkage). Among these alternatives, Ward's linkage is the most widely used as it aims to minimize the variance within clusters, that is, the within-cluster sum of squares—which can be considered the other side of the coin of within-cluster homogeneity (Ward, 1963). Ward's linkage therefore is based on the relationship between cases in each cluster rather than the relationship between cases across clusters by considering how the variance within the clusters would be altered by changing their agglomeration. The agglomeration process starts by considering the distance between any two cases so that the two nearest cases are merged into a group. The algorithm proceeds by calculating the distance between the new group and any other case/group, and the two closest groups are combined into a new group. These steps are iterated until the desired number of clusters is obtained.

---

[3] An alternative option to hierarchical clustering based on a generalization of the k-means clustering is the extension of self-organizing maps (SOMs) to longitudinal categorical data based on the results of an OM analysis. This has been proposed in order to preserve the information about the proximity or opposition between the clusters, as the SOM method is at the same time a classification method and a nonlinear projection method that locates groups in a two-dimensional grid via a dissimilarity matrix based on a Euclidean dissimilarity measure (Massoni et al., 2009). A detailed presentation of this method is beyond the scope of this book, but it is worth mentioning it as it offers objective (data-driven) criteria (proximity/ opposition) to compare clusters qualitatively.

The nested structure emerging from the hierarchical clustering algorithm can be displayed using a dendrogram. Figure 4.2 shows the dendrogram from the application of the Ward algorithm to family formation trajectories from our illustrative example. The figure should be read from the bottom, where the initial 1,886 individual sequences represented by the vertical bars are barely visible because of the large sample size. The vertical bars correspond to clusters, while the horizontal bars correspond to the average dissimilarity within the clusters agglomerated at each step. The higher the values on the y-axis, the higher the variance within the cluster. While clusters at the very bottom (the extreme case of individual sequences being

Figure 4.2   Dendrogram based on hierarchical clustering algorithm for family formation trajectories

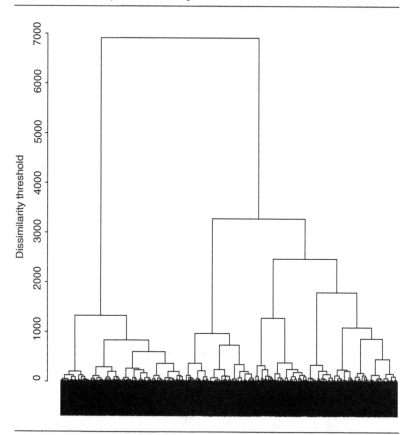

Note: Ward's linkage and nonsquared dissimilarities; OM costs are *indel* = 1 and substitution = 2.

considered as clusters with only one case) have the lowest within-cluster variance, the two clusters at the very top have the highest.

4.1.3 Partitional Clustering

Partitional approaches generate a cluster solution with a fixed number of clusters specified ex ante. The algorithm is based on an iterative procedure. The process is initiated by setting the desired k number of groups and by (arbitrarily) selecting k cases as the reference case for each cluster. This reference case can be the centroid (k-means approach) or the medoid (k-medoid or partitioning around medoids approach; see Kaufman & Rousseeuw, 2005). The centroid is calculated as the mean dissimilarity between all cases assigned to the cluster, meaning that it does not have to correspond to an observed case in the cluster. On the other hand, the medoid is an actual case that is selected at the end of the iterative procedure because the sum of distances to all other cases in a cluster is minimized.

More precisely, the process starts with the random assignment of cases to the k groups initially set. The first reference case is randomly identified for each group. The algorithm assigns the other cases to the groups based on their dissimilarity to the clusters' reference cases in an iterative procedure. In each iteration, all pairwise dissimilarities are considered to find the optimal reference case for the successive iterations until there is no change in the allocation of the sequences to the clusters. Compared to hierarchical clustering, partitional clustering offers the advantage of maximizing a global criterion rather than a local criterion and allows for faster computation because the comparison is to the reference cases only rather than between all cases. Moreover, the identified clusters do not overlap as much as in hierarchical clustering, where all lower level clusters are part of higher level groups. However, partitional approaches have some drawbacks. Indeed, they require an a priori specification of the k groups so that different initial partitions can result in other final clusters.[4] Moreover, the final solution depends greatly on the starting (reference) cases, but this can be easily addressed by setting an initialization criterion (e.g., by using k groups obtained by running a hierarchical clustering on the same data first; Nie, 2016). Finally, in the case of k means, outliers can dominate the computation of the average.

Note that both the centroid and the medoid are intrinsically related to the dissimilarity measure: Different dissimilarity criteria can lead to different centroids/medoids and, therefore, to the identification of different

---

[4] This is undoubtedly a serious issue. Yet with highly structured data, and when the variability of the process is limited (e.g., when the alphabet is composed of a few states and/or the sequences are not excessively long), the probability of obtaining dramatically different clusters starting from a different number of groups is very low.

typologies. This confirms the importance of taking the analytical steps related to the choice of the dissimilarity criterion seriously.

4.1.4 Using Cluster Quality Indices to Choose the Number of Clusters

Cluster analysis is a powerful data-mining tool, but as Halpin and Chan (1998) have indicated, "cluster analysis will always give a solution even if there is no meaningful structure in the data" (p. 112). As highlighted earlier, it is therefore important for researchers to refer to a series of tools to back up their own choice of the number of clusters. Table 4.1 summarizes the most widely used cluster quality indicators (CQIs) for within-cluster homogeneity and between-cluster separation (Studer, 2013).

Before describing them in more detail, we wish to outline some considerations that are necessary to interpret the values of the CQIs correctly.

Table 4.1 Summary of (selected) cluster quality indicators

	Abbreviation	Interval values	Better value	Interpretation
Average silhouette width	ASW	[−1; 1]	Maximum	Coherence of the assignment: high coherence indicates high between-group dissimilarity and high within-group homogeneity
Point biserial correlation	PBC	[−1; 1]	Maximum	Ability of the clustering to reproduce the original dissimilarity matrix
Hubert's gamma	HG	[−1; 1]	Maximum	Ability of the clustering to reproduce the original dissimilarity matrix (order of magnitude)
Calinski-Harabasz index	CH	[0; ∞]	Maximum	Pseudo F computed from the dissimilarities (more appropriate in its squared version)
Pseudo R^2	R2	[0; 1]	Maximum	Share of the discrepancy explained by the clustering

Note: Adapted from Studer (2013), where a formal explanation of each CQI can be found on p. 32-34.

First, strictly speaking, CQIs cannot be considered tools for statistical validation because the "true" structure of the data is unknown (Warren et al., 2015), but also because the cluster membership is the outcome of a process aimed at simplifying and therefore optimizing the information on complex data rather than being a fixed characteristic of a case in the data (Helske et al., 2021).

Second, no clear-cut thresholds exist to assess whether a given cluster solution has a strong or a weak structure. Unlike in standard cluster analysis, where such thresholds exist, when working with sequences, the thresholds might be meaningless because sequences are highly complex objects. In fact, the CQI values are affected by the length of the sequences and the dimension of the alphabet: the longer the sequence and the larger the alphabet, the higher the probability of obtaining CQI values that point to a weaker data structure. This is certainly a crucial piece of information that should not be disregarded, but it does not directly imply that the clusters are not substantively interesting and informative in light of the theoretical framework.

Third, because clear-cut thresholds do not exist, the values of the CQIs can only be compared across typologies based on the same data set and the same dissimilarity matrix (Studer, 2021). This has two important implications: First, it is meaningless to compare across cluster solutions based on different dissimilarity matrices on the basis of the CQI values, and second, it is highly problematic to compare cluster classifications based on different data sources (see Section 4.3).

Finally, small variations in the values of the CQIs when comparing different cluster solutions should be interpreted with caution, partially due to the aforementioned issue related to the complexity of using sequences as cases for the cluster analysis (Studer, 2021).

In light of these considerations, CQIs have to be regarded as part of a heuristic for validation (discussed in more detail in the last section of this chapter) that the researcher needs to interpret in addition to (and together with) substantive reasoning about the plausibility of the typology—that is, considerations on whether the extracted typology is meaningful with respect to the research question and the expectations based on the theory. We recommend considering such indices jointly, as they generally point to a reasonable range of solutions that can be further analyzed and compared. For example, researchers should make use of as many visualization tools as possible to learn about the structure of the clusters depending on the number of groups extracted, as this is of crucial importance when seeking to make informed decisions that do not rely just on the values of the CQIs.

The average silhouette width (Kaufman & Rousseeuw, 2005) assesses the coherence of case assignments to each cluster based on the dissimilarity of each sequence to the center of the cluster it has been assigned to (accounting for homogeneity) and the dissimilarity to the center of the closest other cluster (accounting for separation). Values close to 1 indicate that the case is more consistent with its own cluster than with any alternative cluster of the selected partition. Conversely, the closer the values are to −1, the more inconsistent that case would be with the cluster. The sequence-specific values are first averaged within clusters (cluster-specific silhouette) and then between clusters to obtain the average silhouette width. The weighted average silhouette width (ASWw) is calculated if the data are weighted to avoid representativity bias (Studer, 2013). Table 4.2 shows orders of magnitude for interpreting this measure as suggested by Kaufman and Rousseeuw (2005). Note, however, that (a) these thresholds were defined for standard cluster analysis, which usually groups cases on the basis of a few variables, and (b) ASW and ASWw tend to favor two-cluster solutions (Henning & Liao, 2013; Studer, 2021). It is therefore not sensible to apply them directly in the context of sequence analysis. As a general heuristic, the dissimilarity matrices derived from complex sequence data produce cluster results that yield rather moderate ASW values.

The point biserial correlation (PBC; see Hennig & Liao, 2013; Milligan & Cooper, 1985) and Hubert's gamma (HG; see Hubert & Arabie, 1985) are referred to as *correlation-based measures* as they account for the ability of the partition to reproduce the original dissimilarity matrix. These indicators are based on the correlation between the original dissimilarity matrix and a newly computed dissimilarity matrix, where pairwise dissimilarities are equal to 0 if the cases are assigned to the same cluster and 1 otherwise. The difference between the two indicators relies on the use of different correlation coefficients. Where PBC computes the Pearson correlation to compare the dissimilarity matrices, HG uses parametric correlations based on order of magnitude (rank). Also in this case, positive values close to 1 indicate good clustering as they stand for high correlation between the

Table 4.2 Orders of magnitude for average silhouette width

ASW	Attempted interpretation
0.71–1.00	Strong structure
0.51–0.70	Reasonable structure
0.26–0.50	Structure is weak (it could be an artifact)
≤ 0.25	No structure

Note: Adapted from Studer (2013).

original and the new dissimilarity matrices, while negative values close to −1 indicate bad clustering. The Caliński-Harabasz (CH) index relies on a pseudo F statistic of the analysis of variance based on the dissimilarities. Limited to Euclidean dissimilarities (and therefore formal distances), it is calculated as the ratio of the sum of between-cluster dispersion and within-cluster dispersion for all clusters—the higher the score, the denser and better separated the clusters. Following Caliński and Harabasz (1974), Studer (2013) suggests drawing on the squared version of the distance matrix when computing the index (CHsq). Pseudo R^2 (R2) indicates the share of discrepancy explained by a given partition (Studer et al., 2011). By definition, this indicator increases as the number of clusters increases, meaning it is not particularly useful to compare different partitions from the same data source; indeed, it is more useful to compare the same number of partitions across different data sources or based on different dissimilarity measures. However, researchers should bear in mind the recommendations made earlier concerning the comparability of cluster solutions.

4.2 Illustrative Application

Here, we apply hierarchical and partitional clustering to family formation sequences. Like in Chapter 3, we use yearly data and an alphabet that combines information on partnership status (single, LAT, cohabitation, or marriage) and the presence of children (no child vs. children, further distinguishing between 1 or 2+ children when married). Because CQIs cannot be used to compare solutions emerging from different dissimilarity matrices, we limit our attention here to the case of a dissimilarity matrix calculated with *indel* = 1 and substitution = 2. Finally, we discuss how to compare solutions based on different time granularity and why to do so.

4.2.1 Hierarchical Clustering: Ward's Linkage

The procedure outlined here applies to any bottom-up-based linkage option. We focus on a widely used method, Ward's linkage, which aims at reducing the within-group dissimilarity. In addition to CQIs, researchers can use a visual inspection of the branches (representing clusters) of the dendrogram (see Figure 4.2) to determine the preferred partition. These branches refer to the changes in the level of dissimilarity due to further agglomerations; the longer the branches before they are rejoined at a higher level, the more dissimilar the two clusters are. A widely used heuristic suggests "cutting" the dendrogram before agglomerations of highly dissimilar clusters. This information is more intuitively displayed in Figure 4.3. A line graph (similar to a scree plot commonly used in the psychometric literature) shows the relationship between the partitions and the dissimilarity thresholds. This heuristic is referred to as the "elbow method," and it identifies the point before which the line begins to flatten, that is, the "elbow." In our example, the most evident elbow is in the correspondence of the transition between a two-cluster and a single-cluster solution.[5] This means that this final agglomeration step would considerably increase the within-cluster dissimilarity compared to earlier agglomeration steps. However, as we go further along the line, other, less evident elbows can be identified, for instance, when moving from a five- to a four-cluster solution.

Figure 4.3   Line graph for the relationship between the number of
clusters and the total within-cluster sum of squared
dissimilarities for family formation trajectories

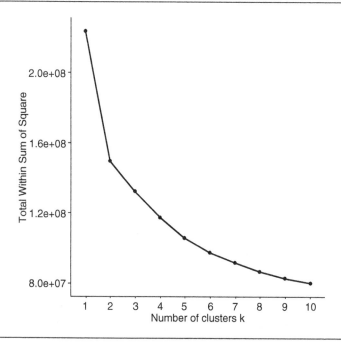

Note: Ward's linkage and nonsquared dissimilarities; OM costs are *indel* = 1 and substitution = 2.

[5] The scree plots can have multiple elbows (also referred to as "knees"), and their identification in many cases is far from objective. We recommend combining this heuristic with more objective measures and the other heuristics for validation discussed in this chapter to determine the number of clusters to extract.

Table 4.3 Cluster quality criteria for output of hierarchical clustering algorithm for family formation trajectories

No. of clusters	PBC	HG	ASW	ASWw	CH	R2
2	0.25	0.30	0.18	0.18	323.97	0.12
3	0.42	0.51	0.21	0.21	293.92	0.20
4	0.53	0.69	0.23	0.23	250.58	0.24
5	0.56	0.74	0.23	0.23	218.61	0.27
6	0.49	0.69	0.16	0.17	193.78	0.29
7	0.51	0.72	0.18	0.18	178.04	0.31
8	0.53	0.77	0.18	0.18	169.58	0.34
9	0.52	0.81	0.16	0.17	167.33	0.36
10	0.52	0.83	0.16	0.17	159.92	0.38

Note: Ward's linkage and nonsquared dissimilarities; OM costs are *indel* = 1 and substitution = 2.

This interpretation is backed up by the CQIs reported in Table 4.3. The ASW values suggest the better solution to be four or five clusters (both 0.23), while the HG and PBC point to five as the best solution. As CH does not have an upper limit, we can only interpret the changes in the slope, which seems to bend more prominently after five clusters.

Notice that the ASW value at 0.23 would indicate "no structure" according to the thresholds displayed in Table 4.2. Given the complexity of the analyzed data, that is, sequences of length 22 time points and a fairly large alphabet distinguishing nine states, we recommend focusing on the relative changes of the ASW values and on the substantive implications of different cluster solutions instead of adhering to benchmarks developed for a different use case. To do so, researchers should first compare alternative partitions to determine which clusters will be merged when moving, in our case, from a five- to a four-cluster solution. Table 4.4 shows this cross-tabulation and reveals that clusters 2 and 3 in the five-cluster solution will be combined in the higher order partition. An option at this point would be to plot the two solutions and consider whether combining the two types represented by clusters 2 and 3 would lead to a loss of information that is actually relevant from a theoretical point of view.[6]

---

[6] See companion webpage for visualizations.

Table 4.4 Comparison of cluster assignments between four- and five-cluster solutions for a hierarchical clustering algorithm for family formation trajectories: Number of cases in each cluster

Five-cluster solution	Four-cluster solution			
	1	2	3	4
1	289	0	0	0
2	0	353	0	0
3	0	147	0	0
4	0	0	386	0
5	0	0	0	691

Note: Ward's linkage and nonsquared dissimilarities; OM costs are *indel* = 1 and substitution = 2.

4.2.2 Partitional Clustering: Partitioning Around Medoids

We focus here on results using the partitional clustering algorithm k-medoid, also known as the partitioning around medoids (PAM) approach (Kaufman & Rousseeuw, 2005). Table 4.5 shows the CQIs for standard PAM, and Table 4.6 shows the CQIs for PAM using the results from Ward clustering (shown earlier) as the initial clustering solution. Focusing on standard PAM, most of the CQIs point to a four-cluster solution as preferable—see Panel a. However, as mentioned earlier, PAM solutions might differ when the algorithm is rerun, as the cases selected to initiate the algorithm are selected randomly each time. For this reason, we consider the CQIs from PAM with the output of a hierarchical clustering using Ward's linkage (Nie, 2016). Results displayed in Panel b indicate that the four- and five-cluster solutions are basically performing equally well, with some indicators favoring one over the other. Note that small differences in the values should be interpreted with caution, meaning that in this case, the researcher should refer to additional heuristics to back up the decision for a specific cluster solution.

One such heuristic is based on a closer consideration of the silhouette values for each case by cluster. In addition, Figure 4.4 offers an overview of the PAM solution with Ward starting points for four and five clusters. Each line in the graph represents the silhouette value of a case with respect to the medoid of the cluster that case has been assigned to; the higher the value, the higher the coherence of that case with the cluster. Therefore, values below 0 indicate a "bad" assignment with respect to that cluster. However, the

Table 4.5 Cluster quality criteria for PAM clustering algorithm for family formation trajectories

No. of clusters	(a) Random initiation of partition						(b) Initiation of the partition based on Ward's linkage clustering					
	PBC	HG	ASW	ASWw	CH	R2	PBC	HG	ASW	ASWw	CH	R2
2	0.42	0.51	0.21	0.21	231.19	0.11	0.43	0.52	0.22	0.23	348.56	0.13
3	0.51	0.63	0.23	0.23	215.14	0.19	0.49	0.61	0.24	0.24	318.83	0.21
4	0.58	0.74	0.25	0.25	201.98	0.25	0.56	0.72	0.25	0.25	272.71	0.26
5	0.48	0.67	0.20	0.20	173.87	0.27	0.57	0.77	0.25	0.25	237.22	0.29
6	0.46	0.68	0.20	0.20	162.08	0.30	0.48	0.71	0.19	0.19	212.05	0.31
7	0.46	0.71	0.18	0.18	149.29	0.33	0.49	0.75	0.20	0.20	200.27	0.34
8	0.50	0.80	0.21	0.22	144.15	0.35	0.50	0.78	0.21	0.21	194.91	0.37
9	0.49	0.81	0.20	0.21	139.62	0.38	0.50	0.81	0.20	0.20	187.59	0.39
10	0.49	0.83	0.20	0.21	131.45	0.39	0.52	0.87	0.23	0.24	184.81	0.42

Note: Nonsquared dissimilarities; OM costs are *indel* = 1 and substitution = 2.

Table 4.6 Comparison between cluster assignments between four- and five-cluster solutions for the PAM clustering algorithm using Ward's linkage clustering starting points for family formation trajectories: Number of cases in each cluster

Five-cluster solution	Four-cluster solution			
	1	2	3	4
1	235	12	2	43
2	54	240	11	21
3	7	232	14	6
4	2	4	266	0
5	0	23	0	694

Note: Nonsquared dissimilarities; OM costs are *indel* = 1 and substitution = 2.

algorithm still considered such an assignment to be preferable on a global level, that is, compared to any alterative option given the number of clusters set up initially. The panel on the left-hand side of Figure 4.4 shows the following information for each cluster (C_j): the silhouette value for all cases, the number of cases allocated to the cluster (n_j), and the average silhouette for the cluster $(ave_{i \in C_j})$. Clusters 3 and 4 exhibit a stronger structure compared to clusters 1 and 2, as, on average, the sequences in these clusters are more consistent with the whole cluster based on the dissimilarity to the medoid. On average, the silhouette values are lower in clusters 1 and 2, where some sequences even have negative values. Looking at the panel on the right-hand side for the five-cluster solution, the last two clusters are highly coherent, while clusters 1, 2, and 3 have low average silhouette values, driven by some negative values and low positive values.

By cross-tabulating the two solutions, we can shed light on the structure of the clusters. That is, we can show how many sequences are consistently assigned to a given group by both cluster solutions and how many sequences exhibit a more fluctuating assignment. The latter sequences are likely to be those with negative silhouette values for the two partitions compared in the cross-tabulation.[7]

---

[7] Cross-tabulations can also be used to compare across cluster assignments by different algorithms, for example, between Ward's clustering algorithm and a PAM clustering algorithm with Ward's starting points.

Figure 4.4 Silhouette values for each sequence by cluster for four- and five-cluster solutions for PAM with Ward's linkage clustering starting points for family formation trajectories

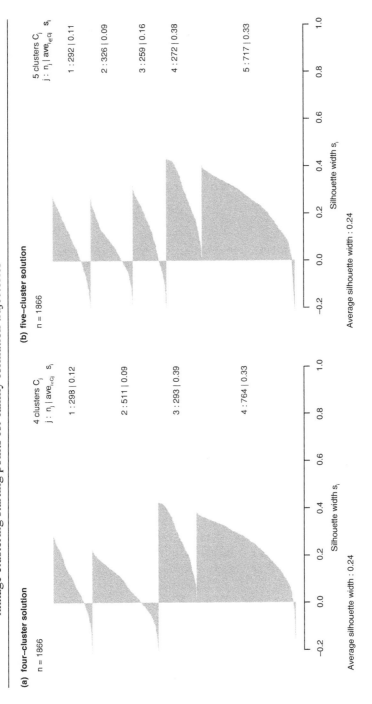

For our illustrative example based on PAM with Ward's linkage clustering starting points, Table 4.6 indicates that three clusters of the four-cluster solution have a strong core of sequences (1, 3, and 4) and that cluster 2 will be affected by a massive reallocation when moving to a five-cluster solution. Looking at Figure 4.4, the cluster-specific average silhouette for cluster 2 in the four-cluster solution is 0.09. As we learned from Table 4.6, this cluster is dismantled to generate clusters 2 and 3 in the five-cluster solution. Figure 4.4 suggests that the cluster-specific average silhouette for the new clusters 2 and 3 are 0.9 and 0.16, respectively. In other words, when choosing the five-cluster solution, we enrich our typology by adding an extra cluster and do not lose anything in terms of average levels of coherence of the assignments of cases to the clusters. Again, visualization tools can further support this decision by clarifying if the five clusters are in accordance with the researcher's theoretical expectations. Figure 4.5 which can be found on the the back of the front cover or at the beginning of the ebook version displays the five-cluster solution using relative frequency sequence plots.[8] Each cluster is visualized by a set of 50 representative sequences (see Chapter 2, Section 2.4.2 for further details). If we had opted for the four-cluster solution, the two types labeled "LAT and long-lasting cohabitation without children" would have been combined in a single cluster with high within-cluster variation in terms of the timing of parenthood. However, these two types resonate with theoretical expectations and prior empirical research on the increasing differentiation of family formation processes as driven by the postponement of parenthood. Therefore, it would be substantively meaningful to retain these two clusters separately. This is a necessarily simplified form of reasoning to justify our choice in this example, but it neatly illustrates that analytical choices should be based on both statistical and substantive considerations. As Figure 4.5 shows, we named the clusters based on a substantive interpretation of the types they represent a color version of this figure can be seen on the inside front cover of the book. We consider a pointed labeling of the clusters another important step serving the primary goal of reducing the complexity of the underlying data. Although such labels partly discount the within-cluster heterogeneity, we encourage researchers to engage with the variability within the clusters when describing them. For example, when looking at cluster 3, it is evident that not all individuals in the clusters marry at the same (early) age; in cluster 4, the characteristic shared by all cases is

---

[8] Although we opted for a simplified visualization and do not complement the relative frequency plots shown in Figure 4.5 with boxplots of dissimilarities to medoids, we strongly recommend always inspecting and including them (at least in an appendix) in regular research papers or reports (see, e.g., Struffolino et al., 2020, and Devillanova et al., 2019). The corresponding boxplots for Figure 4.5 are shown on the companion webpage.

long-lasting singlehood, but in several instances, individuals were in LAT relationships. These are pieces of information that a researcher ought to convey when describing these clusters.

Comparison Between Solutions Based on Different Time Granularity

In the previous example, we relied on yearly time granularity. To emphasize the importance of making a theoretically grounded decision on what time granularity to use when multiple options are available, we compare results for a five-cluster solution based on yearly data (as before) and on monthly data. In both cases, the dissimilarity matrix is computed based on OM with *indel* = 1 and substitution = 2. However, because the sequences are qualitatively different (as, for example, the monthly data are likely to show a higher number of transitions between states), the pairwise dissimilarity matrices will not be identical. In fact, in our illustrative example, the two matrices have correlations equal to -0.32. Therefore, we cannot assume that we will obtain the same cluster assignment for the two dissimilarity matrices, although the obtained cluster solutions might be similar. Table 4.7 shows the cross-tabulation between cluster assignments based on yearly and monthly data for a five-cluster solution.

Indeed, most cases are on the main diagonal—indicating agreement in assignment—but the table also displays a notable share of off-diagonal cases. This illustrates that groupings can differ to a great extent when moving from yearly to monthly granularity, although they are, strictly speaking, based on

Table 4.7 Comparison of cluster assignments based on yearly and monthly data for the five-cluster solutions for the PAM clustering algorithm with Ward's linkage clustering starting points for family formation trajectories: Number of cases in each cluster

Yearly data	Monthly data				
	1	2	3	4	5
1	222	38	7	3	22
2	91	108	115	11	1
3	0	35	212	11	1
4	5	29	2	263	0
5	2	217	5	0	493

Note: Nonsquared dissimilarities; OM costs are *indel* = 1 and substitution = 2.

the same data source. For example, cluster 2 constructed from monthly data is a combination of clusters 2 and 5 based on yearly data, while cluster 2 based on yearly data is a combination of clusters 1, 2, and 3 based on monthly data. As with the previous examples, we recommend complementing the tabular inspection of the results with a visualization that provides a better understanding of the substantive differences between the two cluster solutions.

To better understand the implications of choosing a clustering algorithm and gain useful information about the data structure, we recommend using a factorial technique that offers a visual representation of a dissimilarity matrix: multidimensional scaling (MDS; see Halpin & Chan, 1998, and Piccarreta & Lior, 2010). The information from the pairwise dissimilarity matrix is translated into points representing sequences that are dispersed in a Cartesian bidimensional space whose coordinates depend on the original dissimilarity between sequences. Cases can then be flagged according to the cluster membership so that the researchers can visually inspect the degree of separation between clusters and the within-cluster homogeneity. For illustrative purposes, we extracted three clusters from our sample of family formation sequences based on two different clustering algorithms; Figure 4.6 displays the dispersion of the cases assigned to the three clusters via hierarchical clustering (left-hand panel) and partitional clustering (right-hand panel). The y- and x-axes correspond to the coordinates of the cases on the two factors extracted via MDS. Each case is flagged depending on the cluster assignment.

We begin by considering cluster 1. According to the hierarchical clustering solution, not only are the black dots more dispersed (low within-cluster homogeneity) but the cluster is generally less well separated compared to the other clusters. With the partitional clustering solution, cluster 1 appears less dispersed (the black dots are, on average, closer to each other, i.e., there is higher within-cluster homogeneity) and the cluster is more clearly separated from the others. All in all, at least for this hypothetical three-cluster solution, partitional clustering seems to be a better option. As we will illustrate in the next section, researchers can use several cluster quality indices together with the visualization tool offered by MDS to choose the final partition.

4.3 "Construct Validity" For Typologies From Cluster Analysis to Sequences

The validation of clustering structures is the most difficult and frustrating part of cluster analysis. Without a strong effort in this direction, cluster analysis will remain a black art accessible only to those true believers who have experience and great courage. (Jain & Dubes, 1988, p. 222)

Figure 4.6 Multidimensional scaling visualization (two factors) for a three-cluster solution based on different clustering algorithms for family formation sequences

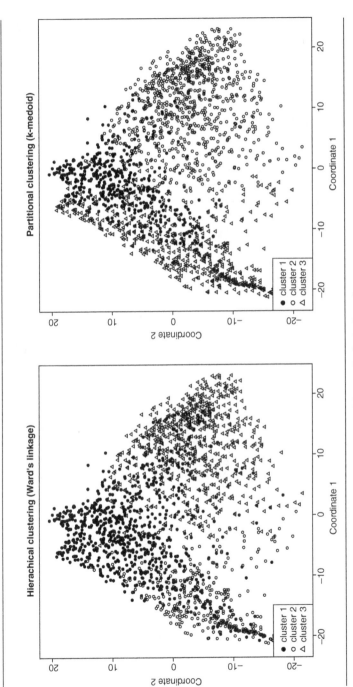

Note: Yearly data; nonsquared dissimilarities; OM costs are *indel* = 1 and substitution = 2.

Although we do not necessarily agree with the pessimism expressed by Jain and Dubes with respect to the difficulty of conducting cluster analysis, we do share their concern that validation remains largely unaddressed for cluster analysis in general. In the context of SA, even when a taxonomy—that is, a natural grouping of sequences—exists, the underlying structure that generated the data is typically unknown (see Warren et al., 2015, for a discussion). This prevents validation in a statistical sense, because the ability of clusters to recover the "true" structure of the data cannot be assessed. On one hand, the quality of a partition (and therefore of the corresponding typology) can be evaluated by referring to several criteria (not necessarily concordant) that can support researchers in making decisions about the specific clustering algorithm to use or the number of clusters to consider. On the other hand, even when a partition is satisfactory from the statistical point of view, there is no guarantee that the identified types will be the most relevant ones from a substantive point of view—that is, with respect to the research question. It is therefore extremely difficult to assess the statistical relevance of a specific solution and the consistency across alternative options (Piccarreta & Studer, 2018; Studer et al., 2011). Thus, SA differs from other methods for longitudinal categorical data analysis (such as event history models, multistate models, or latent Markov models) that are part of the statistical variable-centered or event-oriented culture and rely on the assumption of a stochastic data-generative process. SA is individual centered: The sequences—which are regarded as realizations of a specific process—constitute the units of analysis and are studied as a whole in their temporal unfolding.

A good typology should do a number of things: It should be generalizable to other observations, generalizable to other properties (variables), and linked to a theory (Shalizi, 2009). In the case of cluster analysis applied to sequence analysis, this implies that, first, if data on the same process are available, the typologies should have some features in common. Second, clusters are meaningful only if they are associated with key external characteristics (Gauthier et al., 2009). It is therefore important to consider whether they are associated with independent variables or outcomes. From a substantive point of view, this is consistent with what we have defined as an "institutional" approach to cluster analysis. From a methodological point of view, the fact that the sequences that belong to the same type have the same association with the baseline characteristics can be interpreted as an indicator of within-cluster homogeneity. Finally, the typology should speak to the theoretical expectations—that is, they have to make sense substantively.

In this section, we outline a nonexhaustive list of heuristics in the spirit of the validation criterion referred to as construct validity, which is "based on the logical and empirical relationship among constructs (Babbie, 1979). Translated to sequence analysis, we can state that if groupings found with sequence analysis relate to variables as theoretically expected, this indicates construct validity" (Aisenbrey & Fasang, 2010, p. 433). In other words, the aim should be to increase our confidence in the plausibility of the results and their theoretical interpretability. Ideally, as many heuristics as possible should be used to gain a deep knowledge of the data, as SA is ultimately a data-driven descriptive method and any typology is, therefore, a construction.

Two closely linked caveats should be taken seriously when seeking to build construct validity: Researchers should not disregard within-cluster heterogeneity and should not overinterpret the typology. As discussed earlier, within-cluster heterogeneity is partially driven by the choices made in previous steps when building the sequences (alphabet, time granularity, length of the sequence, dissimilarity measure, etc.).[9] It is therefore important to base choices on substantive reasoning and perform multiple tests on the substantive implications of each step for identifying a final typology.

Visualization tools remain key when inspecting the clusters' structure, especially those that display sequences (rather than the distribution of states over time) and minimize overplotting. Organizing sequences within clusters according to a substantive criterion (e.g., the timing of occurrence of a specific state) is useful to visualize patterns. Another ordering criterion that can point to the presence of subgroups within the clusters is MDS (Piccarreta & Lior, 2010), which is an underused tool with great descriptive potential.

Partitional clustering can give rise to the misleading impression that a cluster can be perfectly summarized by its most central sequence (centroid or medoid). Such a strategy would neglect the dispersion around the representative sequences, which could easily be uncovered, for example, by inspecting the silhouette values. Acknowledging the within-cluster heterogeneity, however, is important to avoid overinterpreting the typology, especially when it is then used as a dependent/independent variable in subsequent analytical steps (see next section).[10]

Finally, Studer (2021) has recently introduced a parametric bootstrap method for cluster homogeneity to measure the extent to which the quality of the obtained typology surpasses the one we would obtain for data with no clustering structure. If this is the case, we can be confident our typology

---

[9] Dlouhy and Biemann (2015) use simulations to assess the share of misallocated sequences across cluster solutions depending on the sample size and the sequence length. Simulations have the advantage of being compared against a known data structure, so it is certainly useful to grasp the orders of magnitude of certain occurrences. In empirical applications based on observational data, the "true" data structure remains unknown.

[10] Piccarreta and Struffolino (2019) have introduced an integrated approach to identify deviant sequences in clusters, distinguishing between structurally peculiar sequences, which have low-frequency features, and sequences with no clear or distinctive characteristics, which can be regarded as random noise (outliers). They borrow from the DBSCAN clustering algorithm (Ester et al., 1996) to identify outliers.

captures a relevant clustering structure when compared with the "null case." This comparison also provides a baseline value for interpreting CQI values and describing their behavior with a varying number of groups (p. 294).

The special case of comparing cluster classifications across different data sources. For several applications in life course research, comparing cluster classifications that are interpreted as typologies of the same temporal process but based on different data sources is of key interest. One typical case is when family formation or employment trajectories are compared across two or more countries where country-specific economic developments and different welfare state systems are regarded as structural driving factors that affect how life courses unfold over time (e.g., Aisenbrey & Fasang, 2017). Comparing typologies implies assessing qualitative differences between sequences of categorical states. Whereas ordinal or cardinal variables such as income can be easily compared across countries because they are measured on a common scale, the matter becomes more difficult in the case of categorical variables, such as a cluster typology (Chang, 2013; Fasang et al., 2019).

Facing the threat of incommensurability, we recommend that researchers carefully consider their analytical choices when comparing sequences across different data sources. Most importantly, we want to highlight the pitfalls that might arise from pooling data from different sources. First, a joint analysis of the data might be hampered by the fact that the data were collected in a different fashion across cases. Retrospective and perspective survey data, for instance, are differently affected by memory bias (Manzoni et al., 2010). In addition, the latter are exposed to sample attrition across survey waves. Other concerns arise from diverging sampling strategies (e.g., oversampling of minority groups) or varying survey modes (face-to-face vs. telephone interview) across data sources. But even if the data were collected within the same framework (e.g., the Gender and Generation Survey [GGS], the Survey on Health Ageing and Retirement and Europe [SHARE]) and are based on standardized procedures and questionnaires, a pooled analysis might be severely affected by varying sample sizes, with larger samples dominating the results (e.g., when working with data-driven substitution costs).

When pooling data sources, sample-specific clusters that are substantively interesting may not emerge because they are not prevalent in other samples and/or because the sample sizes are different across cases and the case with the largest sample will tend to "drive" the identification of clusters that are pertinent to it. Another difficulty arises if certain states do not appear in all samples (e.g., the state mandatory military service in career trajectories). While those states might be very relevant within a case-specific analysis, their role might be discounted in a pooled analysis, particularly if those states are observed in only a small subset of the pooled data. At the same time, rarely observed states that appear in only a few subsamples might hinder the identification of the most central patterns in a joint analysis of all data sources. Finally, a pooled analysis should be considered problematic if a given state of the alphabet has different substantive (social) meanings across contexts. In view of these concerns, we recommend closely inspecting the idiosyncrasies of each sample separately before considering a joint analysis (Fasang et al., 2019).

Fuzzy Clustering

Crisp/hard clustering algorithms rely on the assumption that the assignment of each case to a group implies its exclusion from the other groups. This assumption is challenged by two issues: first, by the lack of formal statistical validation of clustering solutions, and second, by the fact that when data display low separation and/or high homogeneity, sequences assigned to different clusters might have extremely low dissimilarity, but the crisp clustering is unable to account for this ambiguity. The idea that cases belong to different groups to different degrees because boundaries between classes of objects are analytical artifacts that do not represent social phenomena appropriately is central to fuzzy set analysis (Ragin, 2000). The intuition of a "fuzzy" membership to social units (e.g., households), especially in the correspondence of transitions along individual life courses, has been developed both conceptually and methodologically in the field of demography (Goldstein et al., 2000; Murphy, 1996). In the case of sequence analysis, the concept of fuzzy versus crisp assignment to groups that allows for the identification of hybrid types has been introduced recently by Studer (2018). This technique computes sequence-specific "membership probabilities" for each cluster and thus allows for identifying hybrid cases that fit equally well into different groups. Unlike previous attempts using fuzzy algorithms that simply identified cases with the group with which they display the highest membership probability, Studer suggests retaining the original fuzzy membership matrix (which reports the membership strength from 0 = min. to 1 = max. for each case in the sample) and using it in a regression framework. He further suggests Dirichlet regression models (Maier, 2014)—an extension of beta regression (Ferrari & Cribari-Neto, 2004)—as the most appropriate method to deal with this kind of data. This proposition is certainly very promising, but no substantive empirical paper using fuzzy clustering in the context of sequence analysis has been published yet. Piccarreta and Struffolino (2021) have introduced a so-called *transparent index plot* to effectively visualize the degree to which each sequence belongs to each cluster.

4.4 Using Typologies As Dependent and Independent Variables in a Regression Framework

Typically, the identification of groups via cluster analysis is motivated by an interest in either understanding what characteristics increase or decrease the likelihood of following a specific temporal pattern represented by the clusters (i.e., clusters' assignment is the outcome) or estimating the effect of having followed a specific temporal pattern represented by the clusters on a variable measured at the end of the observational window (i.e., cluster assignment is a predictor). This can be pursued by estimating regression models.

When using clusters as variables in a regression analysis, it is important to keep in mind that the clusters usually summarize temporal processes, so they can be conceived as time-constant variables. Accordingly, the regression models should include only covariates measured either prior to and at the onset of the sequences (when clusters are the dependent variable) or at the end of the sequences and afterwards (when clusters are the independent variable). Variables measured at a time point occurring along the sequences should not be included in the model, as they should be considered endogenous to the process captured by the cluster variable.

In Chapter 7, we present a series of advances that allow for accounting for time-varying covariates in the models by combining SA and event history analysis. Within the standard SA framework, time-varying covariates can be included only if they are considered when specifying the states of the alphabet. Suppose that we want to estimate the association between a typology of partnership trajectories and life satisfaction at the end of the observational window. Although prior research has shown that partnership status and life satisfaction are related to the presence of children, it would be incorrect to add this variable to the model because childbirth is likely to have occurred along the sequence. However, as the parenthood trajectory is crucial for life satisfaction in later life and fully observed in our data, we could incorporate the time-varying information on the number of children in the sequence by modifying the alphabet accordingly (combination of partnership and parental status).

Finally, a word of caution is necessary given the discussion on validation of cluster analysis. It is true that the cases assigned to a cluster are assumed to have full membership with respect to that cluster and null membership with respect to the other clusters—irrespective of the degree of dissimilarity with the medoid or the rest of the sequences in the cluster. This assumption implies that the link between the sequences in a cluster and any antecedent or outcome variable is the same within clusters. The earlier discussion demonstrated that this is a strong assumption: Several sequences are highly dissimilar to the medoid (or centroid) of the cluster or from most sequences in the cluster depending on the homogeneity of the data structure. These very sequences might display different values on the covariates compared to those that are closer to the medoid or less dissimilar to one another.

We recommended that researchers should (at least) closely scrutinize the clusters visually and also monitor the characteristics of the cases assigned to each group. Let us consider our illustrative example. One cluster is characterized by long-term singleness, where 90% of the individuals remain single until age 40 and 10% eventually marry. Although all sequences share the feature of long-term singleness, the 10% who eventually got married might have baseline characteristics that substantially differ from those of the 90% who remained single. The role this 10% will play when using the clusters in regression analyses is not given ex ante, so it is crucial to gain a compound knowledge of the clusters in terms of their baseline characteristics and the degree of heterogeneity of the sequences therein to avoid misinterpretations. A nonsignificant regression coefficient, for instance, could be caused by the aggregation of highly heterogeneous sequences to a common cluster. The "true" associations thus might be masked by an incoherent clustering. For the sake of simplicity, in what follows we assume clusters to be homogeneous enough in terms of both the processes summarized by the clusters and the value of sequences on regressors. For real-world applications, we recommend performing as many robustness checks as possible to back up such assertions.

4.4.1 Clusters as Outcomes

Before considering the results from the multivariable models, it is good practice to look at the marginal distribution of all covariates across clusters (column % in Table 4.8) and the cluster "profiles" by each covariate (row % in Table 4.8). For the sake of brevity, we now focus on our main covariate of interest. The row percentages convey one important piece of information: Although the distribution of those born in East Germany across clusters 2 to 5 approximately mimics the distribution in the sample, East Germans represent 42% of those assigned to cluster 1, "Early parenthood in different partnership types," while among West Germans, the relative proportion of individuals following this pathway is lower in comparison to the average percentage of West Germans in the sample (58% vs. 77.1%). This suggests that the pattern represented by cluster 1 might have been more relevant in East Germany overall. This is confirmed by looking at the column percentages: One fourth of the East Germans in the sample experienced a pathway characterized by early parenthood in different partnership types, and another one fourth had a pathway characterized by early marriage with 2+ children. This latter pattern is also highly prevalent among West Germans (36%), while the former is only experienced by 9% of West Germans in the sample. No differences or only very minor ones appear with respect to the other three clusters.

Table 4.8 Descriptive distribution of covariates across clusters and cluster profiles for family formation trajectories

Cluster	Within Cluster %		Across Cluster %		Total %	
	East	West	East	West	Mean	N
1. Early parenthood in different partnership types	42.0	58.0	25.7	9.2	17.5	292
2. Postponed marriage and parenthood	17.7	82.3	17.2	20.7	19.0	326
3. Early marriage with 1 child	20.1	79.9	11.2	11.5	11.4	259
4. Long-lasting singleness and childlessness	19.2	80.8	19.9	21.6	20.8	272
5. Early marriage with 2+ children	15.5	84.5	26.1	36.9	31.5	717
Total						
Mean	*22.9*	*77.1*				
N	*658*	*1,208*				*1,866*

Note: Weighted.

Because clusters as an outcome are a categorical variable with more than two values, we estimate a multinomial logistic regression for the probability of being in each of the five clusters extracted as a function of having been born in East or West Germany. Our data set includes a series of variables that we can use to adjust the model. Specifically, we include gender and education (having obtained a high school certificate or not) in the model. We estimate predicted probabilities for cluster membership by our main covariate of interest because the interpretation of odds ratios or logit coefficients in multinomial logistic regressions is not straightforward. Table 4.9 shows the predicted probabilities and the 95% confidence intervals. Having been born in East or West Germany only makes a difference to the likelihood of having experienced a specific family formation process in the case of cluster 1 and cluster 5: Keeping other covariates at their mean, those born in East Germany were more likely than those born in West Germany to follow the pattern characterized by "Early parenthood in different partnership types," while the opposite applies to the pattern of "Early marriage with 2+ children." For the other clusters, estimates are not significantly different, confirming what we detected when looking at the descriptive distributions.

Table 4.9 Predicted probabilities and confidence intervals (95%) for the assignment to family formation clusters by geographical area of birth: East and West Germany

Cluster		Predicted probability	Lower C.I. 95%	Upper C.I. 95%
1. Early parenthood in different partnership types	East	0.25	0.21	0.29
	West	0.09	0.08	0.11
2. Postponed marriage and parenthood	East	0.18	0.15	0.22
	West	0.21	0.19	0.23
3. Early marriage with 1 child	East	0.11	0.09	0.14
	West	0.12	0.11	0.14
4. Long-lasting singleness and childlessness	East	0.19	0.15	0.22
	West	0.19	0.17	0.21
5. Early marriage with 2+ children	East	0.27	0.23	0.31
	West	0.38	0.36	0.41

Note: The model includes gender (men/women) and high school certificate (yes/no).

4.4.2 Clusters as Predictors

Similarly, when using clusters as independent variables, it is good practice to consider the value of the dependent variable across clusters. In our example, we treat satisfaction with family life (values from 0 to 10) measured at the end of the observational window covered by the sequences as a continuous dependent variable. Table 4.10 shows that, for most clusters, the mean satisfaction with family life is relatively high but with some variation that might be due to compositional effects. We therefore estimate a multivariable model to identify statistically significant differences across clusters after adjusting for confounders.

The choice of modeling strategy depends on the distribution of the outcome variable. In our case, we opted for a linear regression model, as alternative strategies that better suit the right-skewness of the distribution of satisfaction with family life give similar results but are more difficult to interpret substantively. Table 4.11 shows the estimates for the association between satisfaction with family life and cluster membership. The model is adjusted for gender, the attainment of a high school certificate, and having been born in East or West Germany. Having postponed marriage and parenthood (cluster 2) is associated with a statistically significantly lower satisfaction with family life (–0.34 points) compared to having experienced early parenthood in different partnership types (cluster 1, reference category). A significantly lower satisfaction with family life (–0.65 points) compared to cluster 1 corresponds to long-lasting singleness and childlessness.

Table 4.10 Descriptive distribution of satisfaction with family life by family formation clusters

Cluster	Mean	Standard deviation	N
1. Early parenthood in different partnership types	8.22	1.72	292
2. Postponed marriage and parenthood	8.08	1.81	326
3. Early marriage with 1 child	8.21	1.89	259
4. Long-lasting singleness and childlessness	7.54	2.19	272
5. Early marriage with 2+ children	8.37	1.59	717

Note: Weighted.

Table 4.11 Association between satisfaction with family life and family formation clusters

	Estimate	Standard error	*P*-value
Cluster (Ref = 1. Early parenthood in different partnership types)			
2. Postponed marriage and parenthood	–0.34	0.16	0.03
3. Early marriage with 1 child	–0.16	0.18	0.36
4. Long-lasting singleness and childlessness	–0.65	0.16	0.00
5. Early marriage with 2+ children	0.07	0.15	0.64
Intercept	8.34	0.14	

Note: The model includes gender (binary), high school certificate (yes/no), East/West Germany (binary).

CHAPTER 5

MULTIDIMENSIONAL SEQUENCE ANALYSIS

In this chapter, we explore different methods for the joint analysis of multiple processes. Social scientists are often interested in the connections between multidimensional temporal processes, that is, distinct processes that occur simultaneously. For example, to understand how physical and mental health trajectories are related, we have to account for them jointly (e.g., Raab et al., 2018). The SA literature usually refers to these simultaneously unfolding processes as channels, domains, or dimensions, which we use interchangeably in the remainder of this book. In what follows, we first introduce the intuition behind multidimensional sequence analysis by using our example data on family formation and labor market trajectories. We outline different methods to account for the multidimensionality of processes: the expansion of the alphabet, the cross-tabulation of groups identified from different dissimilarity matrices, the combination of domain-specific dissimilarities, and multichannel sequence analysis (MCSA).[1] Especially in the case of MCSA, exploring the correlation between the domains is a crucial step that is extensively addressed in Section 5.5.

5.1 Accounting for Simultaneous Temporal Processes

The simultaneous analysis of different temporal processes can aim at both exploring the descriptive relations among domains and using these interdependencies to generate joint rather than marginal results (Piccarreta, 2017). For instance, in life course applications, we can better understand the temporal dynamics of family trajectories if we incorporate information on the temporal dynamics of employment trajectories, and vice versa (e.g., Aisenbrey & Fasang, 2017). Analyses of such interdependencies have challenged traditional optimal-matching-based approaches (OM) and promoted the idea of a holistic account of temporal processes

---

[1] We use the umbrella term *multidimensional* sequence analysis for consistency with the literature, where dimensions refer to different domains to be accounted for jointly (e.g., different life course domains such as family formation and labor market participation) rather than to dimensions in a statistical sense. Probably a more appropriate term for this family of sequence analysis methods would be "multiprocess" (but this would not be consistent with the literature) or "joint sequence analysis," as suggested by Piccarreta (2017).

(Gauthier et al., 2010; Han & Moen, 1999; Pollock, 2007). In fact, in critiques of the first wave of SA applications, one of the crucial shortcomings identified was the limited capacity of classical OM to account for the unfolding of processes in different, interdependent domains (Levine, 2000; Wu, 2000). The next section is devoted to the presentation of methods currently available to account for simultaneous temporal processes: the expansion of the alphabet, the cross-tabulation of groups identified from different dissimilarity matrices, the combination of domain-specific dissimilarities, and multichannel sequence analysis.[2] It is important to note that these strategies can be pursued only if the channels refer to processes that occur at the same time, that is, they are synchronous (e.g., housing tenure and health trajectories for the same individual from age 18 to age 45). We illustrate how to apply them, examining the interdependence of family formation and labor market trajectories using monthly data covering ages 18 to 40 years. As in previous chapters, we use an alphabet that combines the partnership status (single, LAT, cohabitation, or marriage) and the presence of children (no child vs. children, further distinguishing between 1 or 2+ children when married) to capture the family biographies. For labor market participation, we distinguish between "education," "military/ civilian service," "part-time," "full-time," "self-employed," "parental leave," "not/marginally employed," and "unemployed."[3]

Researchers who wish to account for multidimensional temporal processes tend to assume that the two (or more) processes are correlated. This assumption should be based on theoretical expectations (Fasang, 2015). However, the (degree of) interdependence between channels representing different domains has to be assessed empirically before any classification technique is applied (Piccarreta, 2017; Piccarreta & Elzinga, 2013). This is important because—as the reader will know at this point—the clustering procedure will always generate a result, even when the groups exhibit high within-group heterogeneity and also when the considered channels are not correlated. We argued, therefore, that every cluster analysis should be based on a thorough understanding of the examined

---

[2] For a strategy to measure dissimilarities between multidomain sequences, see Robette and colleagues (2015).

[3] Those defined as not employed are not officially registered as unemployed, and here they are considered similar to those marginally employed; that is, those who work for only a few days in the month. In contrast, those defined as unemployed are officially registered as such and entitled to unemployment benefits, but they are also expected to apply for jobs, participate in trainings offered by the employment office, and accept job offers.

processes and the implications of analytical choices made throughout the research process. Examining multidimensional sequences requires additional steps for obtaining such knowledge, which we will discuss at the end of the chapter.

5.2 Expanding the Alphabet: Combining Multiple Channels Into a Single Alphabet

The expansion of the alphabet implies that the two or more channels and their alphabets are combined to end up with one alphabet and hence one channel (Aassve et al., 2007; Struffolino et al., 2016). Expanding the alphabet efficiently accounts for the co-occurrence of states across different domains over time, but it can easily result in a very large alphabet of states. The states we used to code our family trajectories are an example of alphabet expansion, as we combined information on the partnership trajectory (single, living apart together, cohabitation, marriage) with the fertility trajectory (no children, one child, 2+ children). The final number of states should have been $4 \times 3 = 12$. In Chapter 2, we discussed why a researcher might want to reduce the number of states by collapsing some of them for theoretical or pragmatic reasons. In our case, the combinations of "single"/"cohabitation"/"living apart together" and "2+ children" were extremely rare. As a result, we reduced the alphabet to nine states. This would have been even more necessary if we had wanted to combine partnership and parenthood trajectories with employment trajectories.

Our example data allow us to distinguish between "education," "military/civilian service," "part-time," "full-time," "self-employed," "parental leave," "not/marginally employed," and "unemployed." An alphabet combining the family formation alphabet used in Chapter 4 and this labor market alphabet would include $9 \times 8 = 72$ states. Note that some combinations may not be observable, because either they are mutually exclusive (e.g., being childless and on parental leave) or they simply do not occur in the analyzed sample. Irrespective of the number of combined states eventually chosen, setting up the cost scheme might raise issues regarding the rationale for assigning specific costs to the *indel* or substitution operations between states, which are hardly substantively comparable. For example, why should substituting "single no children + education" with "single no children + part-time" cost more or less than substituting "single no children + full-time" with "married no children + full-time"? Finally, when combining states from different channels, we do not know the specific contribution of each state combination to the computation of pairwise dissimilarities (Cornwell, 2015; Gauthier et al., 2010).

5.3 Cross-Tabulation of Groups Identified From Different Dissimilarity Matrices

Alternatively, the researcher may keep the different channels separate and conduct an OM analysis on each channel independently.[4] In this instance, a dissimilarity matrix would be calculated for each channel and then used as input for a classification method (e.g., cluster analysis) to identify a typology. The joint distribution of the resulting typologies could then be explored by a simple cross-tabulation. Although this is relatively easy to implement, the procedure has two major flaws. First, it does not account for the interdependence of the channels directly, as the channels are modeled independently. Second, the cross-tabulation might identify groups that are sparsely populated, so that the descriptive power and the parsimony of the emerging typology might be compromised (Gauthier et al., 2010). Table 5.1 shows the cross-tabulation for a five-cluster solution on both channels obtained from separate OM and cluster analysis (note, however, that it is also possible to extract a different number of clusters for each channel). In this case, several cells are indeed sparsely occupied, and even when focusing on the most populated ones, we would have to elaborate on many combinations and justify why we disregard the others.

Table 5.1 Cross-tabulation for a five-cluster solution on family formation and labor market channels obtained from separate cluster analyses

Labor market trajectory	Family formation trajectory				
	1	2	3	4	5
1	152	71	86	93	108
2	36	3	75	22	25
3	25	10	31	17	12
4	12	10	14	8	4
5	83	34	29	35	32

Note: OM dissimilarities matrices computed for the two channels separately; costs are *indel* = 1 and substitution = 2 for both channels.

---

[4] In this case, choices with respect to the *indel* and substitution costs can differ across the channels depending on substantive considerations as discussed at the beginning of this chapter.

5.4 Combining Domain-Specific Dissimilarities

Instead of running separate cluster analyses for each channel, one could also combine the dissimilarity matrices prior to clustering (Han & Moen, 1999). The joint dissimilarity matrix can be created using different arithmetic operations. Table 5.2 shows the pairwise dissimilarity values for three illustrative sequences displayed in Figure 5.1, which are computed separately for each channel, as well as two joint dissimilarity matrices obtained by summation or averaging. Both strategies change the relationships between the sequences relative to the initial distance based on one channel. Whether this makes sense from a substantive point of view depends on the

Table 5.2 Dissimilarity values between three sequences referring to three individuals extracted from the initial sample and the family formation and labor market channels

Separate dissimilarity matrices

	Family formation				Labor market		
	Sequence 1	Sequence 2	Sequence 3		Sequence 1	Sequence 2	Sequence 3
Sequence 1	0	40	34	Sequence 1	0	28	26
Sequence 2	40	0	22	Sequence 2	28	0	10
Sequence 3	34	22	0	Sequence 3	26	10	0

Ex-post joint dissimilarity matrices

	Summation				Average		
	Sequence 1	Sequence 2	Sequence 3		Sequence 1	Sequence 2	Sequence 3
Sequence 1	0	68	60	Sequence 1	0	34	30
Sequence 2	68	0	32	Sequence 2	34	0	16
Sequence 3	60	32	0	Sequence 3	30	16	0

Note: OM dissimilarities matrices computed for the two channels separately; costs are *indel* = 1 and substitution = 2 for both channels.

research question and the data structure. However, "this approach disregards the cost needed to simultaneously align the set of sequences (one for each domain [channel]) characterizing one individual with the set of sequences characterizing another" (Piccarretta, 2017, p. 256), meaning that it might represent a suboptimal strategy in many cases.

5.5 Multichannel Sequence Analysis

This strategy consists of computing the dissimilarity between two cases by adapting the substitution and *indel* costs "so that they reflect the relationship between the two [*or more*] channels" (Gauthier et al., 2010, p. 10).[5] Instead of a single cost scheme as for single-channel SA, multichannel sequence analysis (MCSA) uses as many as the channels considered, and these cost schemes are used to align individual sequences pairwise at each point in time in the different channels simultaneously. For a formal presentation of the algorithm's steps, we refer the reader to Gauthier and colleagues (2010). The purpose of this introduction to the method highlights that the dissimilarity between two individuals' sequences in two domains is not obtained by averaging ex post the dissimilarity value calculated on the two (or more) domains as in Table 5.2, but by averaging the alignment costs at each point in time in the two (or more) domains. Strictly speaking, the clusters identified on the basis of the dissimilarity matrix computed by using this strategy represent the relation between the specific domains' states and dissimilarities rather than the association between domains (Piccarreta, 2017).

Based on theoretical considerations, researchers may want to (a) give a different weight to one of the channels so that the differences between sequences in the channel with higher weight contribute more to the clustering, and/or (b) set different substitution and *indel* costs for each channel.[6] Similar to the strategies outlined earlier, the alphabets for the different channels are defined independently of each other. The procedure requires the channels to be represented by sequences that are of the same length, have the same time scale (e.g., months or years), and have the same temporal window (e.g., from ages 18 to 40).

---

[5] While the other methods for multidimensional SA can be applied by using any dissimilarity measure, for MCSA only those presented in Chapter 3 can be used (that is, only those that Studer & Ritschard, 2016, define as "edit distances" that use state-dependent substitution costs).

[6] Note that although both the standard SA of a single channel and the MCSA produce the same output—a dissimilarity matrix—MCSA requires some extra attention if the dissimilarities are used in further analysis (see Chapter 4).

Before running an MCSA, exploring if and to what extent two (or more) domains are correlated should represent the first step of any multidimensional SA to be able to give an accurate and reliable substantive interpretation of the results. We provide a relatively intuitive presentation of a selection of heuristics to explore the correlation between domains by using family formation and labor market trajectories from pairfam. This real-data example aims at demonstrating how complex (and sometimes ambiguous) the decision-making process can be when it comes to applying MCSA. We encourage the reader to approach the original publications (e.g., Gauthier et al., 2010; Piccarreta, 2017; Pollock, 2007) for a more technical presentation of the statistical aspects and further illustrative examples. Moreover, we want to highlight that this subfield of SA is relatively new and rapidly developing. Thus, we ask the reader to keep an eye on forthcoming advances in this domain that might complement the material covered in this section.

The first heuristic refers to the test of a linear association between the two channels, that is, between the two dissimilarity matrices computed on each channel separately.[7] Piccarreta (2017) suggests using the Mantel coefficient to calculate the correlation between all possible pairwise dissimilarities. A positive Mantel coefficient indicates that small pairwise dissimilarities in one domain correspond to small pairwise dissimilarities in the other domain, and vice versa, and that the dissimilarities in the two domains increase together. By contrast, a negative Mantel coefficient indicates that cases that are similar on one channel are dissimilar on the other. For our illustrative example, we computed channel-specific dissimilarity matrices on sequences using yearly data with the same parameters for both channels (OM, *indel* = 1 and substitution = 2)—but note that these can be tuned differently for each channel. We obtain a Mantel coefficient value of 0.05 (with 100 repetitions, to obtain a simulated p-value, which in our case corresponds to 0.01). This is not a very high correlation, but we have to bear in mind that the Mantel coefficient is a test of linear correlations and that these might be obscured if dissimilarities are correlated differently across subgroups within the analyzed data. For instance, in our example data, it is plausible to expect gender-specific associations because, in the case of Germany, family trajectories have been shown to be more connected to employment trajectories among women (Aisenbrey & Fasang, 2017). Therefore, we also calculated the Mantel coefficient for men and women separately: Women's labor market and family formation trajectories exhibit

---

[7] As an alternative to the linear Mantel correlation, Piccarreta (2017) suggests using rank-based correlation coefficients (e.g., the Spearman coefficient) for monotone relation between dissimilarities.

Figure 5.1 Pseudo R^2 and the average silhouette width across number of clusters for the (a) family formation and (b) labor market channels and for the (c) joint dissimilarity matrix from multichannel sequence analysis

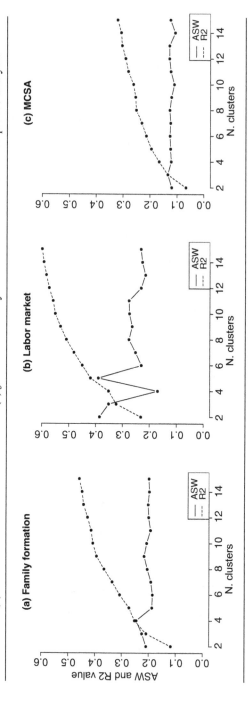

Note: Nonsquared dissimilarity matrices; OM costs are *indel* = 1 and substitution = 2.

a correlation of 0.13, while for men it is only 0.02. This might suggest that, in an actual empirical application, the researcher should consider conducting separate analyses by gender to avoid overlooking gender-specific dynamics in the link between family formation and labor market trajectories. Alternatively, a low Mantel coefficient—that is, a lower linear correlation between channels—might be explained by the existence of a one-to-many association between channels. In this case, we can expect one type of family trajectory to be associated with two types of labor market trajectories. Finally, as anticipated earlier, the condition requiring that dissimilarities in the two domains increase together to a linear correlation to be detected refers to the relation between states and dissimilarities, not the relation between domains. As a consequence, the chosen substitution costs might (partially) mask the association between domains as measured by the correlation between the dissimilarities. We refer to Piccarreta (2017) for advanced techniques to evaluate the association among domains (based on Cronbach's α and principal component analysis).

The second heuristic is based on a comparison of the cluster analysis results obtained by performing separate cluster analyses for each channel to the results of a cluster analysis conducted within the context of an MCSA. Similarly to the first heuristic, it aims at uncovering potential nonlinear relations between domains. Following Piccarreta and Elzinga (2013) and Piccarreta (2017), we do so by comparing the average silhouette width (ASW) and the pseudo R^2 (R2) values across domain-specific partitions and joint domain partitions. When multiple channels are used to build a joint typology, the question arises of whether a typology based on a common dissimilarity matrix represents all considered channels equally well. As in our illustrative case, the channels might differ in terms of the number of states in the alphabet and the overall variability of the process. Usually, we can assume that the channel with the higher variability (in terms of either number of states or occurrence over time of the states) is likely to dominate the results of the cluster analysis because the clustering algorithm will end up maximizing the differentiation between the sequences of the most variable channel. This implies that the clusters will be more similar to each other in terms of the other sequence channel(s). Consequently, a joint analysis faces the risk of discounting differences within the less dominant channels, which would be visible in an analysis that examines the channels separately.

Panel a in Figure 5.1 suggests that a five-cluster solution (or alternatively a three-cluster solution) would be preferable for the labor market channel (see the two peaks in the ASW and the two elbows in the R2). Panel b shows that, for the family formation channel, four and nine clusters would be the local optima. Panel c is based on the joint dissimilarity matrix, computed by averaging the substitution and *indel* costs needed to align the sequences in each channel. For the joint matrix, both the R2 and the ASW indicate three- and nine-cluster solutions as optimal. As expected, the ASW value for this matrix is lower than those in Panels a and b due to the higher complexity of the data. This means that if we strictly follow the recommendation of the R2 and the ASW and opt for a three-cluster solution, we might overlook some types in both the labor market and the family formation channels that would allow us to maximize the separation between the groups and the within-cluster homogeneity. On the other hand, if we opt for a nine-cluster solution, we might end up with multiple clusters that differ very little from one another, and this will compromise a meaningful substantive interpretation of the results. Figure 5.1 provides us with another very important piece of information: On average, the ASW values of the preferred solutions for the labor market channel are much higher (see values on the y-axes) than those for the family formation channel. This means that, for the latter, the types will be more similar to each other. Hence, we can expect the labor market channel to drive the classification emerging from a joint analysis of the two channels.

Visualizations of the different typologies are required to substantiate these considerations and justify the final decision on the number of clusters. This way, it becomes apparent which types would be disregarded if opting for a parsimonious cluster solution with, for instance, three rather than nine clusters. Visualization is also the basis for the last heuristic we recommend using. Before any partitioning into clusters is undertaken, it is advisable to inspect the channels to gather information about the prevalence of states over time and to get a sense of the overall within-channel variability. For this, we can draw on the visualization tools introduced in Chapter 2. We recommend sorting sequences using multidimensional scaling (Piccarreta, 2017) in the sequence index plots for obtaining an accessible overview of within-channel variability and recognizing groups of similar sequences in the data.[8]

We found that the linear correlation between the two channels in our illustrative example is not very high, so we use these data to perform an MCSA by calculating the combined pairwise dissimilarity matrix, and we interpret the results in light of the heuristics outlined earlier.

---

[8] For further details on the descriptive use of multidimensional scaling, see Piccarreta and Lior (2010), who proposed a graphical approach to visualize the relation between two channels via multidimensional scaling, as well as Piccarreta and Elzinga (2013), who introduced criteria to quantify the strength of the possible association, and Piccarreta (2017), who extends Piccarreta and Lior (2010) to more than two channels. The companion webpage offers different visualizations for the two channels where sequences are sorted according to the multidimensional scaling of one channel at the time. The resulting plots can be compared to Figure 5.2.

We assigned the same weight to both channels and also used identical transformation costs for the OM (*indel* = 1; substitution = 2). The cluster quality indices are displayed in Table 5.3. As discussed earlier, the values are relatively low compared to the single-channel CQIs. As we recommended not overinterpreting small differences, Table 5.3 is not very informative because the values are highly similar across different cluster solutions. However, we can combine the insights obtained by applying different heuristics to support a final decision on the cluster partition.

We know, for instance, that the best partition for the labor market trajectory would be a five-cluster solution; four clusters would be optimal for the family formation trajectory (see Figure 5.1). As a first step, we plot the channels using multidimensional scaling on the family formation trajectories as an ordering criterion (see companion webpage) and learn that the labor market channel exhibits lower within-channel variability. More than one third of the sequences are characterized by an early transition from education to full-time work, followed by stability in this latter state for the whole observational window. By contrast, the variability in the family formation channel is higher, which is partly caused by the larger alphabet. To consider how much substantive information we gain by relying on a four- or a five-cluster solution, we should visualize and compare the two options and make a final decision on the basis of one's theoretical expectations. In fact, these two solutions are equivalent according to Table 5.3, but Figure 5.1 highlights that the four-cluster solution might lead to higher within-cluster similarity and higher

Table 5.3 Multichannel sequence analysis: Cluster quality indicators for PAM clustering algorithm with Ward's linkage clustering starting point

No. of clusters	PBC	HG	ASW	ASWw	CH	R2
2	0.22	0.25	0.12	0.12	88.87	0.07
3	0.41	0.51	0.13	0.13	95.32	0.13
4	0.37	0.48	0.12	0.12	78.44	0.16
5	0.35	0.49	0.12	0.12	67.84	0.18
6	0.34	0.49	0.11	0.11	60.81	0.20
7	0.37	0.57	0.11	0.12	58.40	0.22
8	0.37	0.61	0.12	0.13	56.48	0.24
9	0.38	0.64	0.13	0.14	55.21	0.26
10	0.36	0.63	0.11	0.12	48.99	0.26

Note: Nonsquared dissimilarity matrix; OM costs are *indel* = 1 and substitution = 2; equal weights for the two channels.

between-cluster dissimilarity for the family formation channel, while this would be the case for the five-cluster solution for the labor market channel. The five-cluster solution is displayed in Figure 5.2 which can be found inside the back cover or at the beginning of the ebook version[9]. When restricting to four clusters (see companion webpage) and considering the family formation channel, cluster 1 (long-lasting cohabitation mostly with children) and cluster 2 (slow transition from cohabitation to marriage with maximum 1 child) are partly blended together in one cluster and partly reassigned to others. We might have substantive reasons why we want to keep these clusters separate, although the associated types for labor market trajectories are highly similar. For example, for a research question that focuses on the emergence of new family formation trajectories that imply long-lasting cohabitation instead of marriage, the theory might suggest that individuals who experience these nontraditional trajectories also have specific labor market trajectories, and that this might be especially the case for women as cohabitation versus marriage might signal a less traditional gender ideology that is reflected in decisions concerning labor market participation over the life course. These theoretical considerations favor retaining the five-cluster solution to detect these very differences in the synchronous unfolding of family formation and labor market trajectories.

Two final points about MCSA should be kept in mind. First, as a matter of fact, an MCSA will possibly perform worse than a channel-specific procedure in identifying channel-specific types that may be substantively interesting. It is important to evaluate whether this loss affects all channels equally or not. In the latter case, the results of the MCSA will be strongly impacted by the structure of one channel at the expense of the others, whose structure will be less likely to emerge in a joint procedure (Piccarreta, 2017). Note that although both standard SA for a single channel and MCSA produce the same output—that is, a distance matrix—the latter requires some extra attention if the distances are used in further analysis. Second, it is important not to overinterpret MCSA results. What the clusters combined in Figure 5.2 show is the co-occurrence of events and simultaneous temporal unfolding of spells over time in the two channels. For our illustrative example, we know that the linear correlation between the two channels is very low (0.05); therefore, we have to be careful in interpreting the relationship between the two channels as a correlation or association. The fact that the variability in the labor market trajectory is low (clusters 1, 2, 3, and 5 look very similar and differ mostly in terms of the timing of

---

[9] As an alternative to this visualization, multidomain sequences can be displayed by using the stacked sequence plot (Helske & Helske, 2019).

parental leave and the time spent in education) provides a further reason for not putting a strong emphasis on the association between the two channels. Note, however, that the fact that the results are driven by one channel should be considered not only a statistical artifact, but also a potentially interesting substantive finding. In our example, the results indicate that similar labor market trajectories can come with rather dissimilar family trajectories. Further analysis using the joint typology as a dependent variable might shed some further light on who sorts into which pattern.

CHAPTER 6

EXAMINING GROUP DIFFERENCES
WITHOUT CLUSTER ANALYSIS

This chapter introduces techniques to examine group differences other than cluster and regression analysis combined in order to study the relationship between explanatory variables and sequences. When we draw on the results of cluster analysis, we are not investigating this relationship directly because cluster analysis expresses the diversity of the sequences by forming a limited number of clusters and only then examining the association with a variable of interest. This parsimonious approach undoubtedly has its merits in the context of exploratory data analysis. Still, it discounts the actual amount of diversity in the sequence data by ignoring the variation of sequences within clusters (see Chapter 4 for a discussion). First, we present a set of tools introduced by Studer and colleagues (2011) to circumvent the somewhat controversial clustering step and allow researchers to measure the relationship between sequences and covariates in a more direct fashion. Instead of extracting latent groups using cluster analysis, these ANOVA-based techniques analyze whether sequences differ across observed groups (e.g., men and women or persons with different educational credentials) by translating the dissimilarity matrix into a measure of discrepancy. This can then be used to study the relationship between sequences and covariates through variance decomposition. Second, we introduce a related approach for examining group differences in sequence data proposed by Liao and Fasang (2021). Both approaches provide little information on the substantive nature of group differences, which can be drawn from using appropriate visualizations. Therefore, the chapter concludes by presenting the implicative statistic (Studer, 2015), a descriptive visualization tool in addition to those introduced in Chapter 2.

6.1 Comparing Within-Group Discrepancies

The concept of discrepancy is the starting point for the discrepancy analysis framework in sequence analysis (SA). The discrepancy can be understood as a measure of variability among a set of given sequences. Put differently, it expresses the average distance to the center of gravity of a given group, which is defined as the (hypothetical) sequence that minimizes the sum of distances to all sequences belonging to the respective group. It is defined as half of the weighted average of the pairwise dissimilarities (Studer et al., 2011, p. 477):

$$s^2 = \frac{1}{2W^2} \sum_{i=1}^{n} \sum_{j=i+1}^{n} w_i w_j d_{ij}^v$$

with w_i denoting the weights of sequence i, W referring to the total sum of weights, d_{ij}^v indicating the dissimilarity between sequences i and j, and v as an exponent, which, according to Studer and colleagues (2011), should be set to 1 for non-Euclidean dissimilarity measures such as optimal matching (OM) and 2 for Euclidean dissimilarity metrics.

The discrepancy measure serves as a starting point for applying the ANOVA toolkit in the context of SA. It is utilized to quantify how much of the variation in the sequence data can be explained by a covariate, but it is also interesting in its own right. It measures the degree of variation between sequences in a group: The more similar the sequences are in a given group, the lower the group's discrepancy score. By contrast, if we had a high discrepancy score, knowing the composition of one sequence within the group would be of little help in predicting what another sequence of the same group looked like.

Within the framework of life course theory, a high discrepancy value would be regarded as an expression of destandardization, indicating that life courses within a society are highly unpredictable (Brückner & Mayer, 2005). Note, however, that this does not necessarily imply that the individual sequences within the society became more unpredictable. The unpredictability within sequences is captured by composite indices, such as complexity and turbulence (see Chapter 2, Section 2.5.2), whereas discrepancy is a between-sequence concept that summarizes the dissimilarity of sequences within a group. As a result, the sequences within a group could very plausibly be highly differentiated but also very similar when compared to each other. In such a constellation, we would observe high complexity or turbulence values along with a low discrepancy score. In many instances, however, high discrepancies are associated with more complex sequences.

Table 6.1 presents discrepancies and complexities for different groups using the family and labor market biographies from our sample data with yearly granularity. The discrepancies differ significantly for five of the six group comparisons. For example, the family biographies of women are more dissimilar to each other than the family biographies of men are to each other. The test statistic for the significance of group differences is derived from a generalized version of the Levene test using permutations. This test strategy was proposed by Studer and colleagues (2011) to assess

Table 6.1 Group comparisons of discrepancies and complexities, sequences for family formation and labor market trajectories

		Region			Gender			High school certificate		
		West	East	P-value[1]	Men	Women	P-value[1]	No	Yes	P-value[1]
Family formation	N	1,208	658		827	1,039		1,115	751	
	Discrepancy	13.80	14.79	0.001	13.67	14.41	0.001	14.84	13.15	0.001
	Complexity	0.33	0.32	0.013	0.33	0.32	0.075	0.31	0.35	0.000
Labor market	N	629	398		506	521		602	425	
	Discrepancy	10.75	10.46	0.507	7.35	12.11	0.001	9.54	10.65	0.011
	Complexity	0.22	0.23	0.200	0.17	0.27	0.000	0.20	0.25	0.000

[1]Discrepancy: Levene test. Complexity: t-test.

whether the within-group discrepancies differ significantly across different groups. It accounts for both the strong correlation of dissimilarities involving the same cases and the fact that distances are not usually normally distributed. Welch's t-test was used to determine whether there are significant differences in the group-specific average complexities. While the family sequence discrepancies among men and women differed significantly, this does not hold for the complexities. That is, among men and women, the family sequences seem to be similar in terms of complexity. Interestingly, the group comparisons of family sequences by region and educational attainment revealed that the significantly higher within-group discrepancies of East Germans and persons without a high school certificate are associated with significantly lower complexities. By contrast, significantly higher discrepancies in the group comparisons of the labor market sequences go hand in hand with significantly higher complexities.

6.2 Measuring Associations Between Sequences and Covariates

6.2.1 Discrepancy Framework—Pseudo R^2 and Permutation F-Test

Although the comparison of group-specific discrepancies provides interesting new insights, the primary purpose of the discrepancy analysis framework is to study the relationship between sequences and covariates without the need for prior clustering. For this purpose, Studer and colleagues (2011) have proposed an ANOVA-like variance decomposition drawing on the concept of the sum of squares for dissimilarity measures. Similar to the discrepancy, it is defined as

$$SS = \frac{1}{W} \sum_{i=1}^{n} \sum_{j=i+1}^{n} w_i w_j d_{ij}^{v}$$

The sum of squares can be computed for each category of a covariate and for the entire sample to calculate the total and the residual within the sum of squares, SS_T and SS_W. The association is then expressed as the fraction of what remains between the sum of squares, $SS_B = SS_W - SS_T$, and the total sum of squares. Using the total and the group-specific discrepancies s_T and s_i, and the total and the corresponding (weighted) group sizes n_T and n_i, we can also write the association as

$$R^2 = \frac{SS_B}{SS_T} = 1 - \frac{1}{s_T} \sum_{i=1}^{G} \frac{s_i n_i}{n_T}$$

This measure expresses the share of the discrepancy that can be explained by a certain covariate. As with the Levene test, in this instance, the statistical significance of the association is determined by a permutation test, producing a generalized version of Fisher's F statistic. Regarding the interpretation of the pseudo=R^2 values, it should be noted that according to Liao and Fasang (2021), these values tend to be very low and lack well-established benchmarks indicating which values should be considered weak or strong associations in the context of sequence analysis.

Continuing our example, Table 6.2 shows how the three covariates are associated with labor market and family formation biographies. Whereas all six simple correlations are statistically significant, only two are also relevant from a substantive point of view. Specifically, gender and education are correlated with the labor market biographies. They explain 9% and 7% of the total discrepancy, respectively.

Studer and colleagues (2011) also proposed a multifactor discrepancy analysis that examines the associations of multiple variables simultaneously. The results of a model of this kind are shown in the third panel of Table 6.2. The full model with three covariates explains 16% of the labor market sequence discrepancy. The estimates shown for the covariates are so-called Type II effects. They show by how much the R^2_{total} would be reduced if the respective variable were removed from the model. Removing gender, for instance, would reduce the R^2_{total} by 0.09. Although the multi-variable approach seems appealing, it must be noted that the Type II approach produces robust results only in the absence of interaction effects and consequently is of limited use in many social science applications.

Table 6.2   Associations of covariates with sequences for family formation and labor market trajectories

	Family formation (simple)		Labor market (simple)		Labor market (multivariable)	
	R^2	p-value	R^2	p-value	ΔR^2	p-value
Region	0.01	0.001	0.01	0.001	0.00	0.001
Gender	0.01	0.001	0.09	0.001	0.09	0.001
High school certificate	0.01	0.001	0.07	0.001	0.06	0.001
					R^2_{total}	
Total					0.16	0.001

Fortunately, two approaches address this problem. The first strategy is a tree-structured discrepancy analysis. In this procedure, proposed by Studer et al. (2011), the sample is partitioned into separate groups (nodes) via recursive binary splits that maximize variation across groups until a predefined stopping criterion is met. At each step, the nodes are split by the variable that yields the highest pseudo R^2. This exploratory stepwise strategy lends itself very well to generating potentially insightful visualizations.

Figure 6.1 presents a visualization of this kind, called the *sequence regression tree*, using state distribution plots to characterize each node's sequences. Unlike in the previous examples, here we used a simplified version of the labor market sequences' original alphabet for the regression tree analysis with the same three covariates. The revised alphabet identifies only five instead of eight labor market states and makes it easier to read the plot without using colors. For the sake of visual parsimony, we applied the stopping rule to halt the growth of the tree after the second round of splits. Although the regression tree is based on a slightly less comprehensive alphabet, the results presented in Figure 6.1 corroborate the findings displayed in Table 6.2. They confirm that gender is the covariate that explains most of the discrepancy (first split with an R^2 of 0.0971). After the first split, the nodes on the second level of the figure represent men (left panel) and women (right panel). Not surprisingly, the two corresponding distribution plots show that compared to men, women's sequences include more years working part-time and on parental leave; both groups seem to spend a similar amount of time in education.

The second split reveals a kind of interaction effect. Both groups are split by their educational attainment. This implies that, for men and women alike, education is more predictive of the labor market sequences than the area they live in (the third covariate in our analysis). It should be noted that the regression tree approach would have allowed for a different splitting variable for the groups. Even though education is the splitting covariate for both groups, the figure reveals an important gender difference that was not evident in the analysis of main effects presented in Table 6.2: Among men, education level explains three times as much of the discrepancy as among women (R^2: 0.134 vs. 0.0416). The corresponding visualization suggests that the lower association for women might be driven by the fact that women are similar in terms of time spent in part-time work and parental leave irrespective of educational attainment.

The second strategy for uncovering interaction effects is more suitable for a tabular presentation of results. It merely requires the researcher to split the sample into multiple subgroups before conducting a discrepancy analysis. The interaction of gender and education, for instance, could be studied by examining the pseudo R^2 for women and men with low and high

Figure 6.1 Sequence regression tree presenting state distribution for labor market trajectories

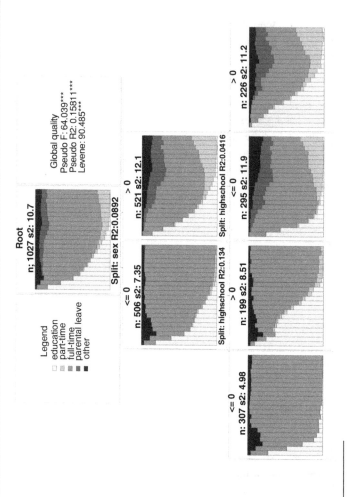

Note: OM dissimilarities matrix; costs are *indel* = 1 and substitution = 2.

education, respectively. Before we turn to the results of these more fine-grained analyses, we first introduce an alternative approach for conducting group comparisons with sequence data. The results of both approaches are presented side-by-side in Table 6.2.

6.2.2 Bayesian Information Criterion and the Likelihood Ratio Test

Partly drawing on the same concepts and following a similar aim as discrepancy analysis, Liao and Fasang (2021) proposed an alternative approach for studying group differences in sequence data. Instead of a permutation test, they apply a likelihood ratio test (LRT) with bootstrapped samples for evaluating the statistical significance of group differences. While permutation methods have the advantage of avoiding distributional assumptions, they are computationally more intensive than the LRT approach.

Like the discrepancy framework, the computation of the LRT can be described as a center-of-gravity approach. It is based on s_i, which is defined as the sum of the squared distances of each sequence j in sequence group i to the center of gravity of the sequence group i.

$$s_i = \sum_{j=1}^{n_i} q_{ij}^2$$

The LRT statistic relates the (weighted) group size adjusted s_i values of the compared groups—for example, men versus women—to the corresponding value of the entire sample, s_A, and is defined as

$$\text{LRT} = n_A \log\left(\frac{s_A}{n_A}\right) - n_A \log\left(\sum_{i=1}^{G} \frac{s_i}{n_i}\right)$$

The test statistic follows a χ^2 distribution, and the degrees of freedom for evaluating the significance are given as $G-1$.

In addition to the likelihood ratio test, Liao and Fasang (2021) proposed using the Bayesian information criterion (BIC) to assess the strength of differences between groups. Applying the same logic as used for the LRT, they evaluate the BIC difference between a restricted model, which assumes that all groups are equal and share a common center of gravity, and an unrestricted model, which allows for group-specific centers of gravity. Drawing on the LRT, the BIC difference can be defined as

$$\Delta \text{BIC} = \text{LRT} - \log(n_A)$$

Liao and Fasang (2021) argue that the BIC difference is preferable to the pseudo R^2 from the discrepancy analysis because the latter often tends to be relatively low and lacks clear benchmarks for evaluating the strength of association. For the BIC difference, however, the literature provides more guidance. Following Kass and Raftery (1995), the level of evidence against the null hypothesis (i.e., no group difference) can be judged according to the cut-off values presented in Table 6.3.

In sum, analyzing group differences using LRT and BIC instead of the discrepancy analysis framework has the advantage of being computationally less demanding and providing somewhat more guidance in assessing the strength of group differences. Moreover, a simulation study by Liao and Fasang (2021) suggests that their approach seems to work better with smaller sample sizes, while discrepancy analysis performs better in assessing the statistical significance of group differences in larger samples. The pseudo R^2, however, tends to decrease with larger sample sizes. Finally, the simulations showed that particularly in settings with small to medium sample sizes (100 sequences in each group), BICs and LRTs were more evenly distributed than the equivalent discrepancy statistics. Based on these results, Liao and Fasang (2021) have suggested evaluating group differences in sequence data by comparing groups of bootstrapped samples of 100 sequences in each group. Although the simulation study revealed many differences between the BIC/LRT approach and the discrepancy framework for some specific scenarios (e.g., small or large sample sizes), both strategies are likely to produce consistent results in many applications because ultimately, both rely on the distances to the group-specific centers of gravity.

Turning to our sample data, Table 6.4 indeed reveals very similar results for both strategies. For instance, the comparison of East and West Germans' labor market biographies results in significant differences in terms of the two test statistics, while both approaches indicate that the observed differences are too small to be substantively meaningful ($\Delta BIC = 0.028$; $R^2 = 0.01$).

Table 6.3 Guidance for interpreting the degree of group differences

ΔBIC	Evidence against H0
0 to 2	Not worth more than a bare mention
2 to 6	Positive
6 to 10	Strong
>10	Very strong

Source: Kass and Raftery (1995).

Despite the absence of relevant differences between East and West Germany for the full sample, Table 6.4 reveals interesting interaction effects that hint at a slightly more nuanced story. The gender differences in the sequences of persons without a high school certificate, for example, are much more pronounced in West Germany (e.g., $\Delta BIC_{East} = 19.91$; $\Delta BIC_{West} = 62.98$). A similar but less pronounced pattern can be seen among individuals with high school certificates.

Overall, the results show that, irrespective of the chosen method, a seemingly simple descriptive analysis as displayed in Table 6.4 can reveal complex interaction effects that involve three or even more variables. The same holds for the regression tree approach demonstrated in Figure 6.1. The latter has the advantage of being particularly well suited to visualizing the results, while the tabular presentation of group differences in Table 6.4 might perform better in meeting the expectations of an audience that is used to making sense of complex regression tables rather than

Table 6.4 Group comparisons using different methods, labor market trajectories

	ΔBIC	LR test p-value	Pseudo R^2	F test (perm.) p-value	N
West vs. East					
Overall	0.01	0.028	0.01	0.001	1,027
Men	3.69	0.013	0.00	0.019	506
Women	0.68	0.018	0.02	0.001	521
Men vs. Women					
Overall	24.85	0.000	0.09	0.001	1,027
West	26.72	0.000	0.11	0.001	629
East	14.41	0.000	0.07	0.001	398
No high school certificate	50.67	0.000	0.12	0.001	602
West	62.98	0.000	0.17	0.001	338
East	19.91	0.000	0.09	0.001	264
High school certificate	17.40	0.000	0.06	0.001	425
West	17.80	0.000	0.08	0.001	291
East	10.09	0.000	0.04	0.001	134

complex visualizations. That said, we consider visualization an essential element of (sequence) data analysis and argue that graphical displays are very helpful—and even essential—if we wish to gain a better understanding of the underlying processes that brought about the group differences shown in a table. This also applies to SA approaches that utilize cluster and regression analysis for analyzing group differences. Compared to cluster analysis, however, the discrepancy framework and the BIC/LRT approach are more parsimonious in terms of their underlying assumptions. Although recent contributions have raised awareness of classification errors and the issue of within-cluster heterogeneity, standard cluster analysis applications usually discount the diversity within clusters and result in deterministic classifications that defy statistical testing. In contrast, the methods presented in this chapter adapt well to the stochastic modeling culture that is still dominant in quantitative social science research. In view of this and the long-standing criticism of classical SA applications, the dominance of cluster-based analyses in the SA literature is somewhat surprising, and we recommend carefully considering the alternative methods outlined here.

6.3 Statistical Implicative Analysis

Although tabular representations of group comparisons, as shown in Tables 6.2 and 6.4, are very informative, the results remain incomplete without a graphical supplement or further group-specific descriptive information on the sequences' characteristics.

This section supplements the techniques for the tabular and visual exploration of sequence data introduced in Chapter 2 by describing a recently proposed tool, the implicative statistic (Studer, 2015). This insightful yet straightforward statistic identifies the typical states at each sequence position for different subgroups. Typical states are identified by comparing the observed distribution of states with the distribution under the independence assumption. The implicative statistic essentially evaluates the degree to which the *membership* in a specific group implies experiencing a specific state at a given sequence position. Indeed, Studer's (2015) software implementation for the TraMineRextras package in R computes the opposite of the implicative statistic, which is defined as

$$I\left(A \rightarrow B\right) = -\frac{n_{\bar{B}A} + 0.5 - n_{\bar{B}A}^e}{\sqrt{n_{\bar{B}A}^e \left(n_{B.} / n\right)\left(1 - n_{.A} / n\right)}}$$

This formula measures the extent to which A implies B by relating the observed number of instances in which the variable of interest does not equal B, $n_{\bar{B}A}$, and the expected frequency of non-B observations under the independence assumption, $n^e_{\bar{B}A}$, to the observed frequencies of A and B, n_B and n_A, and the total number of cases, n. The statistical significance of this statistic is determined by using the adjusted residuals of the underlying contingency table while applying a continuity correction. As the implicative statistic is computed at every sequence position for each state of the alphabet and every considered group, it is not very well suited for use in a tabular presentation but clearly has its merits when it comes to visualization.

Figure 6.2, for instance, is based on $22 \times 5 \times 2 = 220$ implicative statistic scores derived from the yearly labor market sequences also used for the regression tree in Figure 6.1. Accordingly, each sequence in the two comparison groups is of length 22, and the alphabet comprises five distinct states. Figure 6.2 displays only positive implicative statistic scores. If a plotted line is above the dashed horizontal line, the statistic is significant at the 5% level. Accordingly, the figure shows that gender differences in labor market biographies level off in the mid-20s, when women are significantly more likely to experience episodes of parental leave and part-time work than men, while men are increasingly overrepresented in full-time employment spells. The figure nicely complements Table 6.3, which showed significant gender differences (ΔBIC = 24.85; R^2 = 0.09) by pointing to the differences in the distributions of states that drive these differences.

Figure 6.2   Implicative statistic for gender differences in labor market trajectories

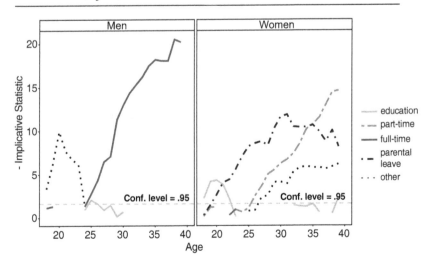

CHAPTER 7

COMBINING SEQUENCE ANALYSIS WITH OTHER EXPLANATORY METHODS

Complementing Chapter 6, this chapter briefly surveys some other recently introduced methodological contributions that aim at bridging the gap between the stochastic and algorithmic modeling cultures. Sequence analysis (SA) is a rapidly advancing field, which makes it nearly impossible to exhaustively summarize recent advances. Therefore, the methods that follow represent a subjective selection of what we consider to be very promising approaches that have already been published in peer-reviewed scholarly journals and that relate closely to the content covered in this volume: the competing trajectories analysis (CTA), the sequence analysis multistate model (SAMM) procedure, and a combination of SA and (propensity score) matching. It would go beyond this introductory book's scope to present these methods in detail. Therefore, we delineate their main features and refer to further literature for an in-depth study of these approaches.

7.1 The Rationale Behind the Combination of Stochastic and Algorithmic Analytical Tools

So far, we have presented SA as an exploratory approach that emphasizes the holistic nature of trajectories. To date, most SA studies have applied this holistic perspective by using a three-stage procedure consisting of the computation of a dissimilarity matrix, a cluster analysis, and a regression analysis in which cluster membership is used as either a predictor or—more commonly—a dependent variable. In Chapters 4 and 6, we showed that this approach rests on some strong assumptions regarding the homogeneity of the obtained clusters. Apart from this issue, however, this procedure suffers from two additional drawbacks: First, it generally requires data with sequences of equal length, because when censored observations are included, there is a risk that the typology obtained by the cluster analysis will be predominantly the result of the varying sequence length. In most cases, this behavior is not desirable from a substantive point of view, it is merely a statistical artifact. Second, using the typology of sequences as a dependent variable in a regression analysis considerably impedes the inclusion of time-varying variables. As a result, such analyses must rely on time-constant covariates that have been measured prior to or at the onset of the sequences. Otherwise, the analysis would suffer from the problem of anticipatory analysis, which occurs when "one attempts to explain *past or current* behavior by *future* outcomes, in other words by conditioning on the future" (Hoem & Kreyenfeld, 2006, p. 462, emphasis in original). Using MCSA (see Chapter 5) to study interdependent processes is not a viable solution to the two problems because it also requires fully observed sequences and examines only the mutual association between sequences but not how a change in one sequence channel affects the other channel. In addition, MCSA is suitable only for incorporating time-varying categorical variables that can be conceptualized as sequences.

In light of these restrictions, a few recent contributions have suggested combining SA and other techniques to overcome these limitations. On one hand, SA has been coupled with event history analysis to study how time-varying variables affect selection into different sequence patterns (Studer, Liefbroer, & Mooyaart, 2018; Studer, Struffolino, & Fasang, 2018). These approaches move away from the holistic perspective of traditional SA by studying transitions into subsequences of shorter length. Thus, the researcher can adopt a more flexible modeling approach with fewer restrictions, but the holistic perspective of the conventional SA approach has to be sacrificed, at least in part. On the other hand, approaches based on different matching procedures have been proposed to establish causal relationships using SA by either balancing the characteristics between treatment and control groups (Karhula et al., 2019; Lee et al., 2017; Raab et al., 2014) or drawing on the results of SA to implement propensity score matching (Barban et al., 2017; Fauser, 2020).

7.2 Competing Trajectories Analysis

CTA is an analytical tool for studying subsequences that come after the first transition following the starting state that all observations share. For the sample sequences we have used so far, this could be the first transition after an unemployment episode or the first change in the partnership trajectory after the end of the first coresidential union. CTA can be divided into two steps. In the first step, the analyst extracts subsequences of a predefined length following a transition of interest. Unlike in the standard SA procedure, this step allows for the inclusion of sequences of unequal length without having to keep an eye on their potentially undesired impact on the results; only the extracted subsequences must be of equal length. This pool of subsequences is reduced to a typology by applying the standard SA procedure of dissimilarity computation and cluster analysis. The second step utilizes a competing-risks event history model instead of an ordinary multinomial logistic regression to estimate the odds of experiencing one of the typical pathways out of the initial state identified in the first step. In contrast to a regular event history analysis, this approach does not study instantaneous transitions (from *time t* to *time t+1*, e.g., from unemployment to employment). Instead, it applies a medium-term conception of change by examining transitions from one state into a subtrajectory comprising multiple consecutive states (Piccarreta & Studer, 2018). For instance, if we were studying subtrajectories spanning 5 years, we might observe that an episode in unemployment ends with a transition to a subtrajectory that starts with a cursory employment spell that lasts only a few months but ends in a stable unemployment spell lasting multiple years. This dynamic would not be captured by a standard event history model focusing on instantaneous transitions. In many cases, this medium-term perspective corresponds to actual decision-making processes in which actors consider not only the immediate consequences of a specific action but also its effect in the foreseeable future. For instance, it might be rational for individuals to decline a job offer when they expect to receive a better one offering more promising career prospects in the upcoming years.

The CTA procedure has several advantages over a conventional combination of sequence, cluster, and regression analysis. First, it allows researchers to analyze how time-varying variables affect the transition into a specific sequence pattern. This is possible because CTA considers the entire period spent in the initial state and allows researchers to add all variables measured during this time as predictors into the competing-risk model estimated in step 2. Second, CTA can handle censored observations and therefore enables researchers to analyze sequences of unequal length as long as the observation period at least matches the length of the extracted subsequences. For instance, if we are interested in the pathways out of unemployment and extract subsequences spanning 5 years, the analysis considers each case that is observed for at least 5 years after the onset of the first unemployment spell. Third, the procedure has positive side effects on the sequence typology obtained in the first step. Since the duration spent in the initial state is not considered in the second stage of CTA, the subsequence patterns are not influenced by timing effects, which otherwise might dominate the pattern identified by the cluster analysis. Moreover, compared to clusters derived from analysis of whole trajectories, the clustering of subsequences usually yields more homogeneous subgroups. As mentioned earlier, these advantages come at the price of relaxing the strict holistic perspective of standard SA by examining only subsequences of medium duration instead of the entire sequence. For further details and an application of CTA, we point readers to the original contribution by Studer, Liefbroer, and Mooyaart (2018), which examines how cultural and economic macro-level changes affect family formation trajectories during young adulthood.

7.3 Sequence Analysis Multistate Model Procedure

The SAMM procedure introduced by Studer, Struffolino, and Fasang (2018) can be conceived as a generalized and more complex version of CTA. It allows researchers to analyze sequences of unequal length and involves a two-step procedure consisting of cluster and event history analysis. In contrast to CTA, SAMM does not focus on one specific transition but extracts all subsequences starting with a transition between two states that are observed for a predefined period, such as all subsequences lasting 5 years that are observed after transitions in employment sequences between ages 18 to 40. If we consider employment trajectories distinguishing the states "employment (EMP)," "education (ED)," and "out of employment (OE)"; observe a sequence A = "(EDU,5)-(EMP,3)-(OE,2)-(EMP,12)"; and want to extract subsequences spanning 5 years, we would obtain the following three subsequences: "(EDU,1)-(EMP,3)-(OE,1)," "(EMP,1)-(OE,2)-(EMP,2)," and "(OE,1)-(EMP,4)." After extracting all subsequences for each starting state (EMP, ED, OE), SAMM then requires conducting separate cluster analyses for every set of subsequences that shares a common starting state. In our example, this would involve three cluster analyses, each yielding its own typology. As the cluster analyses are carried out separately, they can give rise to typologies with different numbers of clusters. The second stage of the analysis involves estimating multistate competing-risk models to study the relationships between (time-varying) covariates and clusters of typical subsequences. In our example, three models would be necessary. In most applications, more than one subsequence with the same starting state can be extracted from the very same sequence, that is, one case can contribute multiple observations to the set of subsequences. The multistate competing-risk models should account for the nonindependence of the observations by adding a frailty term or a random intercept.

Given that SAMM is basically a generalized version of CTA, it shares the same advantages. Compared to CTA, it allows for a more flexible and comprehensive modeling strategy because it considers all possible transitions between the states of the alphabet. This comes at the price of more complexity when estimating and interpreting results. Indeed, applying SAMM might require a reduction in the size of the alphabet in order to make such an estimation strategy feasible. For a more detailed discussion of the peculiarities of the SAMM procedure, we refer to the initial application and the surrounding methodological discussion presented by Studer, Struffolino, and Fasang (2018). In their example, they demonstrate the benefit of SAMM compared to a traditional SA approach by examining how time-varying variables capturing both microlevel and macrostructural change affect women's employment trajectories.

Overall, the combination of SA and event history modeling broadens the analytical scope of SA by linking the exploratory approach of SA with the more explanatory focus of transition rate models. The capacity of this combination to consider time-varying variables makes it considerably easier to study causal relationships between different processes, although the identification of causal effects using transition rate models of course rests on additional assumptions, which are discussed elsewhere (Blossfeld et al., 2019).

7.4 Combining SA and (Propensity Score) Matching

When seeking to establish causal relationships using SA, the combination of SA and event history analysis is not the only approach. A few recent contributions have introduced novel research designs applying different types of matching procedures with a view to balancing characteristics between the treatment and control groups. Raab and colleagues (2014) and Karhula and colleagues (2019), for instance, applied exact matching when comparing the life courses of sibling and unrelated dyads to assess if the higher degree of similarity among siblings is reduced when conditioning on observable background characteristics. Accordingly, they compared only unrelated and sibling dyads who were identical in terms of the covariates considered in the matching procedure. In a similar fashion, Lee and colleagues (2017) used propensity score matching to compare the residential trajectories of low-income households in the United States "that formed their households in public housing or private, site-based assisted housing [and] low-income households that started in nonsubsidized, market-rate housing" (p. 848). As in the previous example, this approach used variables measured prior to or at the onset of the sequences to match the comparison groups.

In contrast, other applications draw directly on the results of SA to implement propensity score matching. Fauser (2020), for instance, first identifies career trajectories using SA and cluster analysis and then estimates the propensity scores for selecting into different career patterns. Based on these propensity scores, she analyzes how different career trajectories relate to cumulative labor market income. Yet another approach has been suggested by Barban and colleagues (2017).

Their article demonstrates how treatment and comparison groups can be balanced by utilizing traditional variable-based propensity score matching, dissimilarities of pretreatment trajectories obtained by optimal matching, and a combination of these two strategies. The authors illustrate their new matching approach in a study of the causal effect of age at retirement on subsequent health trajectories. They use the dissimilarities obtained by SA to match retirees with the most similar health trajectories. In terms of covariate balancing, their newly proposed SA-based matching procedure yielded very similar results to traditional propensity score matching using time-invariant covariates for predicting selection into the treatment. Not surprisingly, a combination of both strategies performs equally well. Overall, these results suggest that a causal matching analysis based on dissimilarities derived from SA can be a viable alternative to standard propensity score matching when the analyzed data do not contain the covariates required to perform a proper regression-based matching. In scenarios in which both identification strategies are possible, they could be combined with or compared to each other in some sort of robustness check.

Taken together, the applications highlighted in this section introduce promising analytical techniques for combining exploratory and explanatory methods within an SA framework. That said, it must be noted that these estimation strategies usually require rather large sample sizes. For instance, three of the five matching studies introduced here draw on large register data containing several thousand observations. Furthermore, the outlined approaches tend to increase the level of methodological complexity by adding steps to the empirical analysis that require researchers to make additional analytical decisions.

While SA scholars are steadily introducing new or more sophisticated methodological tools, SA is increasingly attracting new users who sometimes struggle to get the basics right, let alone implement the latest advances. Against this background, we conclude the book with some recommendations for researchers using tools from the standard SA toolkit before pointing to further recent advances and ongoing developments in the SA literature.

CHAPTER 8

CONCLUSIONS

We conclude the book by first providing practical recommendations that cover all the analytical steps undertaken in typical sequence analysis (SA) projects; however, given the wide range of possible applications of SA, these recommendations do not apply to all projects. Therefore, they should be treated with the necessary level of flexibility. Second, we outline some open issues and ongoing debates in SA that call for/contribute to advances in the field. A compound presentation of all advances is beyond the scope of this chapter because in the past two decades, the field has developed quickly to address those open issues, the community of practitioners has grown, and the propositions of creative combinations of SA with other methods have increased.

8.1 Summary of Recommendations: An Extended Checklist

We defined SA as a toolkit for describing and finding regularities in a set of sequences of events or ordered social processes. We maintained that an SA typically implies many analytical choices that should be theoretically informed and based on a clear research question. At the same time, we acknowledged that SA has traditionally been conceived as an exploratory procedure and a representative of the algorithmic modeling culture. Accordingly, SA consists of deductive and inductive elements that are also reflected in our considerations. While we argue that the analytical choices generally should be made based on theoretical considerations, we also argue that researchers should take advantage of SA's exploratory capabilities, which make it possible to refine existing theories and require researchers to reassess earlier analytical choices based on the results obtained throughout the analysis. An accurate description can emerge only from a deep knowledge of the raw material and from a theoretically informed application of the available tools. We regard this recursive process as a valuable feature that can improve the quality and reliability of the final results as it encourages researchers to carefully contemplate each decision by constantly thinking about the theoretical relevance of what they have done in the previous steps.

Following the outline of the book and based on our personal experience of applying SA, we conclude this volume by providing a list of recommendations that should be considered when conducting a sequence analysis.

8.1.1 Define, Describe, and Visualize the Sequences

- Always consider carefully how your choices might affect the results. The definition of the start and end points, along with the length of the sequences, necessarily has an influence on the outcomes of your analysis. If you do not collect the sequence data yourself, your options might be restricted, but even then, you can usually define the observation window in various ways. In many applications that combine SA with cluster analysis, the identified patterns are driven by group differences in the timing of the first event; this particularly applies in scenarios in which all observed sequences share the same starting state (Studer, Liefbroer, & Mooyaart, 2018). Depending on the research question, this behavior might be desirable or problematic. If it is deemed problematic, it could be addressed by shifting the starting point of the observation period. In a similar fashion, the homogeneity of the extracted clusters is often negatively correlated with the length of the sequences. Again, this is not necessarily a problem, but it is something you should be aware of when making your analytical choices.

- Start big when defining the alphabet. While an alphabet that is too large might impede the identification of well-defined patterns, an alphabet that is too small increases the risk of overlooking meaningful differences. In general, we consider the latter the bigger problem. We therefore recommend starting with a large alphabet that could easily be reduced in the course of the analysis if it seems necessary. That said, the definition of the alphabet should be guided first and foremost by theoretical considerations.

- Be careful when working with sequences of unequal length. In general, we advise against conducting an SA with sequences of unequal length because the results of such analyses are often largely driven by the fact that not all cases are observed for the same period. For applications in which unequal sequence lengths reflect meaningful and substantive differences, this might be a desirable outcome. Often, however, varying sequence lengths indicate some sort of missing data problem—nonresponse, left or right censoring—rather than conveying insightful information. In these cases, you should either restrict your sample to sequences of equal length (complete case analysis) or consider some sort of imputation strategy. It must nevertheless be noted that, despite some promising advances, imputation procedures are not yet well established in the SA literature.

- Make use of the wide range of tools for exploring sequence data. We conceive of SA as an iterative process that relies on a solid knowledge of the analyzed data. Sequence data are inherently complex and contain a plethora of information that is sometimes not easy to extract. Although it might be tempting to proceed to the explanatory part of the analysis, we strongly encourage you to take full advantage of the many descriptive and visual tools of the SA toolkit first. Do not restrict yourself to just inspecting simple descriptive characteristics (e.g., number of episodes, duration spent in each state of the alphabet), but also consider the more complex indicators (e.g., turbulence, entropy) and visualization tools presented in this volume.

- Be aware that SA does not necessarily require dissimilarity computation. In Chapter 2, we introduced several composite indices that aim at providing information on either the duration and sequencing or the "quality" of the states occurring within sequences. These measures are often used for descriptive purposes, but some recent studies have demonstrated their full potential and placed them at the center of their analysis. Note, however, that some of the composite measures might be unduly complex and that simple descriptive indicators might be easier to interpret (Pelletier et al., 2020).

8.1.2 Computing Sequence Dissimilarities

- Make sure that your choice of the dissimilarity measure (alignment- or nonalignment-based) and your cost specification (*indel* and substitution costs) reflect your analytical goals. Ask yourself whether you want to put more emphasis on timing, sequencing, duration, or the qualitative differences between states and compute the dissimilarities accordingly. Assess the performance of your analytical choices by comparing different specifications. For this purpose, we recommend inspecting the obtained dissimilarities among a (carefully selected or even manually created) subset of sequences that reflect the differences you are interested in. For instance, if your main goal is to identify timing differences, you should consider inspecting a subset of sequences containing similar states in a similar order but at different positions (time points) along the sequence. If you compare dissimilarity measures based on these sequences, you will get a first impression of their sensitivity in the detection of timing differences.

- Carefully contemplate which sequence comparison approach is most suitable for answering your research questions. To date, most applications of SA are based on dissimilarity matrices that compare every sequence with every other sequence in the data. However, dissimilarities can also be computed by just comparing specific sequence pairs (e.g., dyadic SA of family members) or by comparing every sequence to a unique or person-specific reference sequence (e.g., when comparing planned or normative behavior with actual behavior).

8.1.3 Clustering Sequences

- Use the cluster quality criteria to guide you in choosing the number of clusters to extract. In general, they allow for an informed choice based on the assessment of the within-cluster homogeneity and between-cluster separation. In many applications, however, the quantitative criteria do not clearly favor one specific solution. Hence, we strongly recommend complementing them with a qualitative assessment based on theoretical expectations to improve the validity of your cluster solution.

- Explore different cluster solutions visually to gain information on the substantive characteristics of the process captured by each cluster. Visualization is key to uncovering differences and similarities between clusters and making an informed decision on what we gain and lose when choosing one cluster solution or the other.

- Do not ignore within-cluster variability; instead, explore the characteristics of those sequences that are highly dissimilar to other sequences in their respective cluster. In some cases, it may be necessary to take a step back and reconsider earlier analytical choices (sequence length, alphabet size, dissimilarity computation) to reduce the share of badly classified cases.

- Be prepared to reconsider prior analytical choices after inspecting your cluster results. In some cases, for instance, the clustering might indicate that rarely occurring states are not relevant enough to have an impact on the results. The results may also suggest that some states of the alphabet tend to capture more or less the same information and therefore do not need to be considered distinct states when defining the alphabet. Likewise, the results might reveal that the chosen dissimilarity measure is ill-specified with regard to a specific feature of the sequences you were initially interested in (e.g., timing or substantive differences). In other instances, the obtained cluster solution may be dominated by the length of the first or last subepisode of the sequences, which—depending on the research question— might warrant a respecification of the sequence length.

- Ensure the validity of your cluster solution before using the typology in subsequent analyses (e.g., clusters as predictors or outcomes in some sort of regression analysis). The validity can be assessed by carefully inspecting quantitative and qualitative criteria and by comparing solutions based on different analytical choices.

- Be aware that your typology represents a simplification of the original sequence data and that the validity of further analysis rests on assumptions regarding the quality of your cluster solution. Do not overinterpret the typology identified via cluster analysis, particularly when—despite all efforts to improve the validity—within-cluster homogeneity and between-cluster separation are low. Note that the degree of homogeneity is likely to vary across clusters. While it is not much of a problem if you obtain a sort of junk cluster comprising heterogeneous sequences, you should be concerned if several clusters show very low within-cluster homogeneity and between-cluster separation. In that case, you should reconsider your previous choices, as the clusters are probably very similar to each other and have limited explanatory power.

- Be careful when using pooled samples consisting of sequences coming from different macrolevel units (e.g., countries). Unit-specific states and patterns might be overlooked when data are pooled together and the same alphabet is used for all units. If the number of sequences varies across units, you run the risk of having larger units dominate the obtained cluster solution; at the same time, some theoretically interesting patterns might remain hidden if they come from units with smaller samples. It is therefore advisable to always approach each unit separately and gain a deep understanding of unit-specific dynamics before deciding to pool samples from different units.

8.1.4 Multidimensional Sequence Analysis

- Explore the linear and the nonlinear correlations between the sequence channels you want to consider jointly. The literature suggests several heuristics based on correlation coefficients, the pseudo R^2, and the average silhouette width to assess the performance of strategies that analyze the channels separately or jointly in terms of the ability to extract the channel-specific clusters that are of substantive interest.

- Be aware that the channel with the higher number of states and/or the higher sequence variability and discrepancy is likely to drive the identification of the typology. Multichannel sequence analysis does not measure how the channels relate to each other in a causal sense, it simply accounts for the co-occurrence of states across channels.

8.1.5 Group Comparisons Without Clustering

- Examining group differences with SA does not require cluster analysis. Although the combination of sequence, cluster, and regression analysis is arguably still the standard procedure in the SA literature, it is possible to study the relationship between sequences and covariates in a more direct fashion using tools such as discrepancy analysis and the implicative statistic. When writing this book, we had the impression that these powerful techniques have been somewhat underused, and we want to encourage our readers to consider them as a sound alternative to the standard procedure.

- When using discrepancy analysis or utilizing BIC comparisons and LRT tests to examine group differences, be aware that these tools only serve to detect and quantify statistically significant group differences. Hence, they should be complemented by analytical tools such as regression trees or a visualization of the implicative statistic—these also provide information on the qualitative nature of the differences.

8.1.6 Added Value of Sequence Analysis

- Proactively assess the added value of your results from SA compared to the standard methods applied in your field. Although SA in the social sciences has a history spanning more than 30 years and has witnessed a rapidly growing body of published research in recent years, its usage still requires more justification than do methods representing the stochastic modeling culture. Simply referring to the holistic process perspective may not be sufficient to convince your audience that you would not have gained the same knowledge by using more established methods. We cannot provide a universal recommendation for addressing such concerns, but based on our own experience, we consider it promising to (a) spell out the added value of SA and (b) demonstrate it empirically if possible. For instance, if you want to use a typology derived from SA as an independent variable for predicting an outcome, you could test whether this approach produces more insightful and better fitting models compared to an approach that just adds specific characteristics of the sequences (e.g., time spent in a certain state or number of episodes) as predictor variables (see Devillanova et al., 2019, as an example of such a strategy).

8.2 Achievements, Unresolved Issues, and Ongoing Innovation

Since its import to the social sciences by Andrew Abbott in the late 1980s, SA has come a long way: The once unconventional method (Koppman & Leahey, 2019) has become a part of the extended toolkit of standard methods within particular subfields—most notably in life course sociology and demography. Like many other methodological innovations, SA was accompanied by controversial debates in which it was heavily criticized. Although some critics might have overstated their case, the methodological debate that culminated in the "2000 controversy" (Aisenbrey, 2017) published in *Sociological Methods & Research* raised awareness for the method and spurred the refinement and extension of the SA toolkit. Many of these newly developed tools that have been described as the "second wave of SA" (Aisenbrey & Fasang, 2010) have been covered in this volume, such as the extensions and alternatives to OM, the heuristics for validation of cluster results, or the computation of composite measures for describing sequences. In certain areas, such as the validation of cluster results or the development of new composite measures, the second wave can be considered a long-lasting one. We still witness a steady inflow of methodological contributions that address the issues raised two decades ago. However, some urgent matters, such as dealing with missing or incomplete data, remained largely unaddressed (with the notable exception of Halpin, 2016a, 2016b).

Despite this unfortunate stagnation in some areas, we highlight that SA is still a relatively young but fast-developing method. This is reflected in the recent methodological advances we conceive as the "third wave of SA." These contributions strive to bridge the gap between the algorithmic tradition of SA and the stochastic modeling culture of standard methods in the social sciences. It was beyond the scope of this book to thoroughly cover these recent developments, as we have focused on providing a solid foundation for conducting a state-of-the-art SA. That said, we briefly showcased some of these tools in Chapter 7, and we conclude this book by referring to further advances in the box and to the book's companion page (which also includes material that has not been covered here). Up-to-date information on advances, methodological discussions, and recent relevant publications can be found on the Sequence Analysis Association webpage (https://sequenceanalysis.org/).

References to Other Advances

We list some additional references pointing to other advances, which indicate rapid and vibrant development in the field of SA.

- Bolano and Studer (2020): Extension of feature selection algorithms to identify the most relevant sequence properties associated with an outcome

- Borgna and Struffolino (2018): Combination of discrepancy analysis and comparative qualitative analysis

- Cornwell (2015, 2018): Network analysis of sequence structures

- Helske et al. (2018), Helske and Helske (2019), and Piccarreta and Bonetti (2019): Combination of hidden Markov models and SA

- Liao (2021): Quantifying and assessing linked trajectories in sequence data

- Murphy and colleagues (2021): Clustering sequences using mixtures of exponential-distance models

- Pelletier et al. (2020): Dynamic SA to measure complexity over time

- Rossignon et al. (2018): Linking event history analysis with SA to estimate the effect of past trajectories on future events

- Studer (2021): Validating SA typologies using parametric bootstrap

- Vrotsou et al. (2014): Similarity measures for event sequences

REFERENCES

Aassve, A., Billari, F. C., & Piccarreta, R. (2007). Strings of adulthood: A sequence analysis of young British women's work-family trajectories. *European Journal of Population, 23*(3–4), 369–388. doi: 10.1007/s10680-007-9134-6

Abbott, A. (1990). A primer on sequence methods. *Organization Science, 1*(4), 375–392. doi: 10.1287/orsc.1.4.375

Abbott, A. (1992). From causes to events: Notes on narrative positivism. *Sociological Methods & Research, 20*(4), 428–455. doi: 10.1177/0049124192020004002

Abbott, A. (1995). Sequence analysis: New methods for old ideas. *Annual Review of Sociology, 21*(1), 93–113. doi: 10.1146/annurev.so.21.080195.000521

Abbott, A. (2017). *Processual sociology.* University of Chicago Press.

Abbott, A., & Forrest, J. (1986). Optimal matching methods for historical sequences. *Journal of Interdisciplinary History, 16*(3), 471. doi: 10.2307/204500

Abbott, A., & Hrycak, A. (1990). Measuring resemblance in sequence data: An optimal matching analysis of musicians' careers. *American Journal of Sociology, 96*(1), 144–185. doi: 10.1086/229495

Abbott, A., & Tsay, A. (2000). Sequence analysis and optimal matching methods in sociology. *Sociological Methods & Research, 29*(1), 3–33. doi: 10.1177/0049124100 0029001001

Aisenbrey, S. (2017). Social sequence analysis: Methods and applications. *Contemporary Sociology: A Journal of Reviews, 46*(6), 665–667. doi: 10.1177/0094306117734868i

Aisenbrey, S., & Fasang, A. E. (2010). New life for old ideas: The "second wave" of sequence analysis bringing the "course" back into the life course. *Sociological Methods & Research, 38*(3), 420–462. doi: 10.1177/0049124109357532

Aisenbrey, S., & Fasang, A. E. (2017). The interplay of work and family trajectories over the life course: Germany and the United States in comparison. *American Journal of Sociology, 122*(5), 1448–1484.

Akkucuk, U. (2011). A study on the competitive positions of countries using cluster analysis and multidimensional scaling. *European Journal of Economics, Finance and Administrative Sciences, 37*, 17–26.

Allison, P. D. (2009). *Fixed effects regression models* (Quantitative Applications in the Social Sciences, Vol. 160). Sage.

Allison, P. D. (2014). *Event history and survival analysis* (Quantitative Applications in the Social Sciences, Vol. 46, 2nd ed.). Sage.

Babbie, E. (1979). *The practice of social research* (2nd ed.). Wadsworth.

Barban, N., de Luna, X., Lundholm, E., Svensson, I., & Billari, F. C. (2017). Causal effects of the timing of life-course events. *Sociological Methods & Research, 49*(1), 216–249. doi: 10.1177/0049124117729697

Basagaña, X., Barrera-Gómez, J., Benet, M., Antó, J. M., & Garcia-Aymerich, J. (2013). A framework for multiple imputation in cluster analysis. *American Journal of Epidemiology, 177*(7), 718–725. doi: 10.1093/aje/kws289

Bernardi, L., Huinink, J., & Settersten, R. A., Jr. (2019). The life course cube: A tool for studying lives. *Advances in Life Course Research, 41*, 100258.

Biemann, T. (2011). A transition-oriented approach to optimal matching. *Sociological Methodology, 41*(1), 195–221. doi: 10.1111/j.1467-9531.2011.01235.x/full

Biemann, T., Fasang, A. E., & Grunow, D. (2011). Do economic globalization and industry growth destabilize careers? An analysis of career complexity and career patterns over time. *Organization Studies, 32*(12), 1639–1663. doi: 10.1177/0170840611421246

Billari, F. C. (2005). Life course analysis: Two (complementary) cultures? Some reflections with examples from the analysis of the transition to adulthood. *Advances in Life Course Research, 10*, 261–281.

Billari, F. C., Fürnkranz, J., & Prskawetz, A. (2006). Timing, sequencing, and quantum of life course events: A machine learning approach. *European Journal of Population/Revue Européenne de Démographie, 22*(1), 37–65. http://link.springer.com/article/10.1007/s10680-005-5549-0

Billari, F. C., & Piccarreta, R. (2001). Life courses as sequences: An experiment in clustering via monothetic divisive algorithms. In S. Borra, R. Rocci, M. Vichi, & M. Schader (Eds.), *Advances in classification and data analysis* (pp. 351–358). Springer. doi: 10.1007/978-3-642-59471-7_43

Billari, F. C., & Piccarreta, R. (2005). Analyzing demographic life courses through sequence analysis. *Mathematical Population Studies, 12*(2), 81–106. doi: 10.1080/08898480590932287

Blanchard, P. (2019). Sequence analysis. In P. A. Atkinson, R. A. Williams, & A. Cernat (Eds.), *Encyclopedia of research methods.* Sage.

Blossfeld, H.-P. (1987). Labor-market entry and the sexual segregation of careers in the Federal Republic of Germany. *American Journal of Sociology, 93*(1), 89–118. doi: 10.1086/228707

Blossfeld, H.-P., & Rohwer, G. (2001). *Techniques of event history modeling: New approaches to causal analysis* (2nd ed.). Psychology Press. doi: 10.4324/9781410603821

Blossfeld, H.-P., Rohwer, G., & Schneider, T. (2019). *Event history analysis with Stata* (2nd ed.). Routledge.

156

Bolano, D., & Studer, M. (2020). The link between previous life trajectories and a later life outcome: A feature selection approach. *LIVES Working Paper*, 82. doi: 10.12682/lives.2296-1658.2020.82

Borgna, C., & Struffolino, E. (2018). Unpacking configurational dynamics: Sequence analysis and qualitative comparative analysis as a mixed-method design. In G. Ritschard & M. Studer (Eds.), *Sequence analysis and related approaches* (pp. 167–184). Springer.

Bouveyron, C., Celeux, G., Murphy, T., & Raftery, A. (2019). *Model-based clustering and classification for data science: With applications in R* (Cambridge Series in Statistical and Probabilistic Mathematics). Cambridge University Press. doi: 10.1017/9781108644181

Breiman, L. (2001). Statistical modeling: The two cultures. *Statistical Science*, *16*(3), 199–231. doi: 10.1214/ss/1009213726

Brückner, H., & Mayer, K. U. (2005). De-standardization of the life course: What it might mean? And if it means anything, whether it actually took place? *Advances in Life Course Research*, *9*(4), 27–53. doi: 10.1016/S1040-2608(04)09002-1

Brüderl, J., Drobnič, S., Hank, K., Nauck, B., Neyer, F. J., Walper, S., Alt, P., Borschel, E., Bozoyan, C., Garrett, M., Geissler, S., Gonzalez Avilés, T., Gröpler, N., Hajek, K., Herzig, M., Huyer-May, B., Lenke, R., Lorenz, R., Lutz, K., Minkus, L., . . . Wilhelm, B. (2019). *The German Family Panel (pairfam). ZA5678 Data file Version 10.0.0.* Cologne. doi: 10.4232/pairfam.5678.10.0.0

Brzinsky-Fay, C. (2007). Lost in transition? Labour market entry sequences of school leavers in Europe. *European Sociological Review*, *23*(4), 409–422. doi: 10.1093/esr/jcm011

Brzinsky-Fay, C. (2014). Graphical representation of transitions and sequences. In P. Blanchard, F. Bühlmann, & J.-A. Gauthier (Eds.), *Advances in sequence analysis: Theory, method, applications* (pp. 265–284). Springer International. doi: 10.1007/978-3-319-04969-4_14

Brzinsky-Fay, C., Kohler, U., & Luniak, M. (2006). Sequence analysis with Stata. *Stata Journal*, *6*(4), 435–460. doi: 10.1177/1536867X0600600401

Bürgin, R., & Ritschard, G. (2014). A decorated parallel coordinate plot for categorical longitudinal data. *American Statistician*, *68*(2), 98–103. doi: 10.1080/00031305.2014.887591

Caliński, T., & Harabasz, J. (1974). A dendrite method for cluster analysis. *Communications in Statistics*, *3*(1), 1–27.

Chang, R. (2013). Incommensurability (and incomparability). In H. LaFollette (Ed.), *The international encyclopedia of ethics* (pp. 2591–2604). Blackwell.

Chavent, M., Lechavallier, Y., & Briant, O. (2007). DIVCLUS-T: A monothetic divisive hierarchical clustering method. *Computational Statistics & Data Analysis*, *52*(2), 687–701.

Chen, S., Ma, B., & Zhang, K. (2009). On the similarity metric and the distance metric. *Theoretical Computer Science*, *410*(24–25), 2365–2376.

Collas, T. (2018). Multiphase sequence analysis. In G. Ritschard & M. Studer (Eds.), *Sequence analysis and related approaches: Innovative methods and applications* (pp. 149–166). Springer International. doi: 10.1007/978-3-319-95420-2_9

Cornwell, B. (2015). *Social sequence analysis: Methods and applications* (Vol. 37). Cambridge University Press. doi: 10.1017/CBO9781316212530

Cornwell, B. (2018). Network analysis of sequence structures. In G. Ritschard & M. Studer (Eds.), *Sequence analysis and related approaches* (pp. 103–120). Springer.

Devillanova, C., Raitano, M., & Struffolino, E. (2019). Longitudinal employment trajectories and health in middle life: Insights from linked administrative and survey data. *Demographic Research*, *40*, 1375–1412.

Dijkstra, W., & Taris, T. (1995). Measuring the agreement between sequences. *Sociological Methods & Research*, *24*(2), 214–231. doi: 10.1177/004912419 5024002004

Dlouhy, K., & Biemann, T. (2015). Optimal matching analysis in career research: A review and some best-practice recommendations. *Journal of Vocational Behavior*, *90*(Supplement C), 163–173. doi: 10.1016/j.jvb.2015.04.005

Elzinga, C. H. (2003). Sequence similarity: A nonaligning technique. *Sociological Methods & Research*, *32*(1), 3–29. doi: 10.1177/0049124103253373

Elzinga, C. H. (2007). *Sequence analysis: Metric representations of categorical time series*. https://citeseerx.ist.psu.edu/viewdoc/download?doi=10.1.1.514.7995&r ep=rep1&type=pdf

Elzinga, C. H. (2010). Complexity of categorical time series. *Sociological Methods & Research*, *38*(3), 463–481. doi: 10.1177/0049124109357535

Elzinga, C. H. (2014). Distance, similarity and sequence comparison. In P. Blanchard, F. Bühlmann, & J.-A. Gauthier (Eds.), *Advances in sequence analysis: Theory, method, applications* (pp. 51–73). Springer International.

Elzinga, C. H., & Liefbroer, A. C. (2007). De-standardization of family-life trajectories of young adults: A cross-national comparison using sequence analysis. *European Journal of Population*, *23*(3–4), 225–250. doi: 10.1007/s10680-007-9133-7

Elzinga, C. H., & Studer, M. (2015). Spell sequences, state proximities, and distance metrics. *Sociological Methods & Research*, *44*(1), 3–47. doi: 10.1177/0049124114540707

Elzinga, C. H., & Studer, M. (2019). Normalization of distance and similarity in sequence analysis. *Sociological Methods & Research*, *48*(4), 877–904. doi: 10.1177/0049124119867849

Ester, M., Kriegel, H.-P., Sander, J., & Xu, X. (1996). A density-based algorithm for discovering clusters in large spatial databases with noise. In E. Simoudis, J. Han, & U. Fayyad (Eds.), *Proceedings of the Second International Conference on Knowledge Discovery and Data Mining* (pp. 226–231). AAAI Press.

Fasang, A. E. (2015). Comment: What's the added value? *Sociological Methodology*, *45*(1), 56–70. doi: 10.1177/0081175015587276

Fasang, A. E., Beduk, S., Büyükkececi, Z., Bastholm Andrade, S., Karhul, A., & Scott, M. (2019, May 2). *Apples and oranges? Comparing life course typologies across countries* [Paper presentation]. SUDA Colloquium, Stockholm, Sweden.

Fasang, A. E., & Liao, T. F. (2014). Visualizing sequences in the social sciences. *Sociological Methods & Research*, *43*(4), 643–676. doi: 10.1177/0049124113506563

Fasang, A. E., & Mayer, K. U. (2020). Lifecourse and social inequality. In J. Falkingham, M. Evandrou, & A. Vlachantoni (Eds.), *Handbook of demographic change and the life course* (pp. 22–39). Edward Elgar.

Fasang, A. E., & Raab, M. (2014). Beyond transmission: Intergenerational patterns of family formation among middle-class American families. *Demography, 51*, 1703–1728.

Fauser, S. (2020). Career trajectories and cumulative wages: The case of temporary employment. *Research in Social Stratification and Mobility, 69*, 100529.

Ferrari, S., & Cribari-Neto, F. (2004). Beta regression for modelling rates and proportions. *Journal of Applied Statistics, 31*(7), 799–815.

Forrest, J., & Abbott, A. (1990). The optimal matching method for studying anthropological sequence data: An introduction and reliability analysis. *Journal of Quantitative Anthropology, 2*(2), 151–170.

Gabadinho, A., Ritschard, G., Müller, N. S., & Studer, M. (2011). Analyzing and visualizing state sequences in R with TraMineR. *Journal of Statistical Software, 40*(40), 1–37. doi: 10.18637/jss.v040.i04

Gabadinho, A., Ritschard, G., Studer, M., & Müller, N. S. (2010). Indice de complexité pour le tri et la comparaison de séquences catégorielles. *Revue Des Nouvelles Technologies de l'information RNTI, E-19*, 61–66.

Gabadinho, A., Ritschard, G., Studer, M., & Müller, N. S. (2011). Extracting and rendering representative sequences. In A. Fred, J. L. G. Dietz, K. Liu, & J. Filipe (Eds.), *Knowledge discovery, knowledge engineering and knowledge management* (pp. 94–106). Springer. doi: 10.1007/978-3-642-19032-2_7

Gauthier, J.-A., Bühlmann, F., & Blanchard, P. (2014). Introduction: Sequence analysis in 2014. In P. Blanchard, F. Bühlmann, & J.-A. Gauthier (Eds.), *Advances in sequence analysis: Theory, method, applications* (pp. 1–17). Springer International. doi: 10.1007/978-3-319-04969-4_1

Gauthier, J.-A., Widmer, E. D., Bucher, P., & Notredame, C. (2009). How much does it cost? Optimization of costs in sequence analysis of social science data. *Sociological Methods & Research*, *38*(1), 197–231. doi: 10.1177/004912 4109342065

Gauthier, J.-A., Widmer, E. D., Bucher, P., & Notredame, C. (2010). Multichannel sequence analysis applied to social science data. *Sociological Methodology*, *40*(1), 1–38.

Goldstein, H., Rashbach, J., Browne, W., Woodhouse, G., & Poulain, M. (2000). Multilevel models in the study of dynamic household structures. *European Journal of Population*, *16*, 373–387.

Gower, J. C. (1971). A general coefficient of similarity and some of its properties. *Biometrics*, *27*(4), 857–871.

Halpin, B. (2010). Optimal matching analysis and life-course data: The importance of duration. *Sociological Methods & Research*, *38*(3), 365–388. doi: 10.1177/0049124110363590

Halpin, B. (2014). Three narratives of sequence analysis. In P. Blanchard, F. Bühlmann, & J.-A. Gauthier (Eds.), *Advances in sequence analysis: Theory, method, applications* (pp. 75–103). Springer. doi: 10.1007/978-3-319-04969-4_5

Halpin, B. (2016a). Missingness and truncation in sequence data: A non-self-identical missing state. In G. Ritschard & M. Studer (Eds.), *Proceedings of the International Conference on Sequence Analysis and Related Methods* (pp. 443–444). Lausanne.

Halpin, B. (2016b). Multiple imputation for categorical time series. *Stata Journal*, *16*(3), 590–612. doi: 10.1177/1536867X1601600303

Halpin, B. (2017). SADI: Sequence analysis tools for Stata. *Stata Journal*, *17*(3), 546–572. http://www.stata-journal.com/article.html?article=st0486

Halpin, B. (2019). Introduction to sequence analysis. In H.-P. Blossfeld, G. Rohwer, & T. Schneider (Eds.), *Event history analysis with Stata* (2nd ed., pp. 282–307). CRC Press.

Halpin, B., & Chan, T. W. (1998). Class careers as sequences: An optimal matching analysis of work-life histories. *European Sociological Review*, *14*, 111–130.

Hamming, R. W. (1950). Error detecting and error correcting codes. *The Bell System Technical Journal*, *29*(2), 147–160.

Han, S.-K., & Moen, P. (1999). Clocking out: Temporal patterning of retirement. *American Journal of Sociology*, *105*(1), 191–236. http://www.jstor.org/stable/10.1086/210271

Healy, K., & Moody, J. (2014). Data visualization in sociology. *Annual Review of Sociology*, *40*(1), 105–128. doi: 10.1146/annurev-soc-071312-145551

160

Helske, S., Helske, J., & Chihaya, G. K. (2021, September 16). From sequences to variables: Rethinking the relationship of sequences and outcomes. *SocArXiv.* doi: 10.31235/osf.io/srxag

Helske, S., & Helske, J. (2019). Mixture hidden Markov models for sequence data: The seqHMM package in R. *Journal of Statistical Software, 88*(3), 1–32.

Helske, S., Helske, S., & Eerola, M. (2018). Combining sequence analysis and hidden Markov models in the analysis of complex life sequence data. In G. Ritschard & M. Studer (Eds.), *Sequence analysis and related approaches* (pp. 185–201). Springer.

Hennig, C., & Liao, T. F. (2013). How to find an appropriate clustering for mixed-type variables with application to socio-economic stratification. *Journal of the Royal Statistical Society: Series C (Applied Statistics), 62*(3), 309–369. doi: 10.1111/j.1467-9876.2012.01066.x

Hepburn, P. (2018). Parental work schedules and child-care arrangements in low-income families. *Journal of Marriage and Family, 80*(5), 1187–1209.

Hepburn, P. (2020). Work scheduling for American mothers, 1990 and 2012. *Social Problems, 67*(4), 741–762. doi: 10.1093/socpro/spz038

Hiekel, N., & Vidal, S. (2020). Childhood family structure and complexity in partnership life courses. *Social Science Research, 87*(102400).

Hoem, J. M., & Kreyenfeld, M. (2006). Anticipatory analysis and its alternatives in life-course research: Part 1: Education and first childbearing. *Demographic Research, 15*(16), 461–484.

Hollister M. (2009). Is optimal matching suboptimal? *Sociological Methods & Research, 38*(2), 235–264. doi: 10.1177/0049124109346164

Hubert, L., & Arabie, P. (1985). Comparing partitions. *Journal of Classification, 2*, 193–218.

Huinink, J., Brüderl, J., Nauck, B., Walper, S., Castiglioni, L., & Feldhaus, M. (2011). Panel analysis of intimate relationships and family dynamics (pairfam): Conceptual framework and design. *Zeitschrift für Familienforschung—Journal of Family Research, 23*(1), 77–101.

Jain, A., & Dubes, R. C. (1988). *Algorithms for clustering data.* Prentice-Hall.

Karhula, A., Erola, J., Raab, M., & Fasang, A. E. (2019). Destination as a process: Sibling similarity in early socioeconomic trajectories. *Advances in Life Course Research, 40*, 85–98.

Kass, R. E., & Raftery, A. E. (1995). Bayes factors. *Journal of the American Statistical Association, 90*(430), 773–795. doi: 10.1080/01621459.1995.10476572

Kaufman, L., & Rousseeuw, P. (2005). *Finding groups in data: An introduction to cluster analysis.* Wiley.

Koppman, S., & Leahey, E. (2019). Who moves to the methodological edge? Factors that encourage scientists to use unconventional methods. *Research Policy*, *48*, 103807.

Kreuter, F., & Kohler, U. (2009). Analyzing contact sequences in call record data: Potential and limitations of sequence indicators for nonresponse adjustments in the European Social Survey. *Journal of Official Statistics*, *25*(2), 203–226.

Kruskal, J. B. (1977). The relationship between multidimensional scaling and clustering. In J. Van Ryzin (Ed.), *Classification and clustering* (pp. 17–44). Academic Press.

Kruskal, J. B., & Wish, M. (1978). *Multidimensional scaling* (Quantitative Applications in the Social Sciences, Vol. 11). Sage.

Lee, K. O., Smith, R., & Galster, G. (2017). Subsidized housing and residential trajectories: An application of matched sequence analysis. *Housing Policy Debate*, *27*(6), 843–874.

Lesnard, L. (2008). Off-scheduling within dual-earner couples: An unequal and negative externality for family time. *American Journal of Sociology*, *114*(2), 447–490. doi: 10.1086/590648

Lesnard, L. (2010). Setting cost in optimal matching to uncover contemporaneous socio-temporal patterns. *Sociological Methods & Research*, *38*(3), 389–419. doi: 10.1177/0049124110362526

Lesnard, L. (2014). Using optimal matching analysis in sociology: Cost setting and sociology of time. In P. Blanchard, F. Bühlmann, & J.-A. Gauthier (Eds.), *Advances in sequence analysis: Theory, method, applications* (pp. 39–50). Springer.

Lesnard, L., & Kan, M. Y. (2011). Investigating scheduling of work: A two-stage optimal matching analysis of workdays and workweeks. *Journal of the Royal Statistical Society: Series A (Statistics in Society)*, *174*(2), 349–368. doi: 10.1111/j.1467-985X.2010.00670.x

Levenshtein, V. I. (1966). Binary codes capable of correcting deletions, insertions and reversals. *Soviet Physics Doklady*, *10*, 707–710. http://adsabs.harvard.edu/abs/1966SPhD...10..707L

Levine, J. H. (2000). But what have you done for us lately? *Sociological Methods & Research*, *29*(1), 34–40. doi: 10.1177/0049124100029001002

Levy, R., Gauthier, J.-A., & Widmer, E. D. (2006). Entre contraintes institutionnelle et domestique: Les parcours de vie masculins et feminins en Suisse. *Cahiers Canadiens de Sociologi*, *31*(4), 461–489. https://www.jstor.org/stable/pdf/20058732.pdf

Liao, T. F. (2021). Using sequence analysis to quantify how strongly life courses are linked. *Sociological Science*, *8*, 48–72.

Liao, T. F., & Fasang, A. E. (2021). Comparing groups of life-course sequences using the Bayesian information criterion and the likelihood-ratio test. *Sociological Methodology*, *51*(1), 44–85. doi: 10.1177/0081175020959401

162

Liefbroer, A. C., & Elzinga, C. H. (2012). Intergenerational transmission of behavioural patterns: How similar are parents' and children's demographic trajectories? *Advances in Life Course Research, 17*, 1–10.

MacIndoe, H., & Abbott, A. (2004). Sequence analysis and optimal matching techniques for social science data. In M. Hardy & A. Bryman (Eds.), *Handbook of data analysis* (pp. 386–406). Sage. doi: 10.4135/9781848608184.n17

Maier, M. J. (2014). *DirichletReg: Dirichlet regression for compositional data in R*. Research Report Series/Department of Statistics and Mathematics, WU Vienna University of Economics and Business, Vienna. http://epub.wu.ac.at/4077/

Manzoni, A., & Mooi-Reci, I. (2018). Measuring sequence quality. In G. Ritschard & M. Studer (Eds.), *Sequence analysis and related approaches* (pp. 261–278). Springer International. doi: 10.1007/978-3-319-95420-2_15

Manzoni, A., Vermunt, J. K., Luijkx, R., & Muffels, R. (2010). Memory bias in retrospectively collected employment careers: A model-based approach to correct for measurement error. *Sociological Methodology, 40*(1), 39–73.

Massoni, S., Olteanu, M., & Rousset, P. (2009). Career-path analysis using optimal matching and self-organizing maps. In J. C. Príncipe & R. Miikkulainen (Eds.), *Advances in self-organizing maps* (pp. 154–162). Springer.

Milligan, G. W., & Cooper, M. C. (1985). An examination of procedures for determining the number of clusters in a data set. *Psychometrika, 50*, 159–179.

Minnen, J., Glorieux, I., & van Tienoven, T. P. (2016). Who works when? Towards a typology of weekly work patterns in Belgium. *Time & Society, 25*(3), 652–675. doi: 10.1177/0961463X15590918

Murphy, K., Murphy, T. B., Piccarreta, R., & Gormley, I. C. (2021). Clustering longitudinal life-course sequences using mixtures of exponential-distance models. *Journal of the Royal Statistical Society: Series A (Statistics in Society), 184*(4), 1414–1451. doi: 10.1111/rssa.12712

Murphy, M. (1996). The dynamic household as a logical concept and its use in demography. *European Journal of Population, 12*, 363–381.

Needleman, S. P., & Wunsch, C. D. (1970). A general method applicable to the search for similarities in the amino acid sequence of two proteins. *Journal of Molecular Biology, 48*(3), 443–453. https://www.sciencedirect.com/science/article/pii/0022283670900574

Nevalainen, J., Kenward, M. G., & Virtanen, S. M. (2009). Missing values in longitudinal dietary data: A multiple imputation approach based on a fully conditional specification. *Statistics in Medicine, 28*(29), 3657–3669. doi: 10.1002/sim.3731

Nie, H. (2016). A new clustering algorithm based on Ward_PAM. *International Journal of Future Computer and Communication, 5*(1), 8–12. doi: 10.18178/ijfcc.2016.5.1.434

Pelletier, D., Bignami-Van Assche, S., & Simard-Gendron, A. (2020). Measuring life course complexity with dynamic sequence analysis. *Social Indicator Research*, *152*(3), 1127–1151. doi: 10.1007/s11205-020-02464-y

Piccarreta, R. (2012). Graphical and smoothing techniques for sequence analysis. *Sociological Methods & Research*, *41*(2), 362–380. doi: 10.1177/0049124112452394

Piccarreta, R. (2015). Comment: Implying sequences using scores—Some considerations. *Sociological Methodology*, *45*(1), 76–81. doi: 10.1177/0081175015588095

Piccarreta, R. (2017). Joint sequence analysis: Association and clustering. *Sociological Methods & Research*, *46*(2), 252–287. doi: 10.1177/0049124115591013

Piccarreta, R., & Billari, F. C. (2007). Clustering work and family trajectories by using a divisive algorithm. *Journal of the Royal Statistical Society: Series A (Statistics in Society)*, *170*(4), 1061–1078. http://onlinelibrary.wiley.com/doi/10.1111/j.1467-985X.2007.00495.x/full

Piccarreta, R., & Bonetti, M. (2019, November 2). Assessing and comparing models for sequence data by microsimulation. *SocArXiv*. doi: 10.31235/osf.io/3mcfp

Piccarreta, R., & Elzinga, C. H. (2013). Mining for association between life course domains. In J. McArdle & G. Ritschard (Eds.), *Contemporary issues in exploratory data mining in the behavioral sciences* (pp. 190–220). Routledge. doi: 10.4324/9780203403020-17

Piccarreta, R., & Lior, O. (2010). Exploring sequences: A graphical tool based on multi-dimensional scaling. *Journal of the Royal Statistical Society: Series A (Statistics in Society)*, *173*(1), 165–184.

Piccarreta, R., & Struffolino, E. (2019, September). An integrated heuristic for validation in sequence analysis. *SocArXiv*, September. doi: doi:10.31235/osf.io/v7mj8

Piccarreta, R., & Struffolino, E. (2021). Enhancing fuzzy clusters' interpretation through visualization. *SocArXiv*.

Piccarreta, R., & Studer, M. (2018). Holistic analysis of the life course: Methodological challenges and new perspectives. *Advances in Life Course Research*, *41*, 100251.

Pollock, G. (2007). Holistic trajectories: A study of combined employment, housing and family careers by using multiple-sequence analysis. *Journal of the Royal Statistical Society: Series A (Statistics in Society)*, *170*(1), 167–183.

Preacher, K. J., Wichman, A. L., MacCallum, R. C., & Briggs, N. E. (2008). *Latent growth curve modeling* (Quantitative Applications in the Social Sciences, Vol. 157). Sage.

Raab, M., Fasang, A. E., & Hess, M. (2018). Pathways to death: The co-occurrence of physical and mental health in the last years of life. *Demographic Research*, *38*, 1619–1634. doi: 10.4054/DemRes.2018.38.53

164

Raab, M., Fasang, A. E., Karhula, A., & Erola, J. (2014). Sibling similarity in family formation. *Demography, 51*, 2127–2154.

Raab, M., & Struffolino, E. (2019). The heterogeneity of partnership trajectories to childlessness in Germany. *European Journal of Population, 36*(1), 53–70. doi: 10.1007/s10680-019-09519-y

Ragin, C. C. (2000). *Fuzzy-set social science.* University of Chicago Press.

Ritschard, G. (2021). Measuring the nature of individual sequences. *Sociological Methods & Research.* doi: 10.1177/00491241211036156

Ritschard, G., Bussi, M., & O'Reilly, J. (2018). An index of precarity for measuring early employment insecurity. In G. Ritschard & M. Studer (Eds.), *Sequence analysis and related approaches* (pp. 279–295). Springer International. doi: 10.1007/978-3-319-95420-2_16

Ritschard, G., & Studer, M. (Eds.). (2018). *Sequence analysis and related approaches.* Springer International. doi: 10.1007/978-3-319-95420-2

Robette, N., & Bry, X. (2012). Harpoon or bait? A comparison of various metrics in fishing for sequence patterns. *Bulletin of Sociological Methodology/Bulletin de Méthodologie Sociologique, 116*(1), 5–24. doi: 10.1177/0759106312454635

Robette, N., Bry, X., & Lelièvre, É. (2015). A "global interdependence" approach to multidimensional sequence analysis. *Sociological Methodology, 45*(1), 1–44. doi: 10.1177/0081175015570976

Rossignon, F., Studer, M., Gauthier, J.-A., & Le Goff, J. M. (2018). Sequence history analysis (SHA): Estimating the effect of the past trajectories on an upcoming event. In G. Ritschard & M. Studer (Eds.), *Sequence analysis and related approaches* (pp. 83–101). Springer.

Sankoff, D., & Kruskal, J. B. (1983). *Time warps, string edits, and macromolecules: The theory and practice of sequence comparison.* Addison-Wesley.

Scherer, S. (2001). Early career patterns: A comparison of Great Britain and West Germany. *European Sociological Review, 17*(2), 119–144. doi: 10.1093/esr/17.2.119

Settersten, R. A., & Mayer, K. U. (1997). The measurement of age structuring and the life course. *Annual Review of Sociology, 23*, 233–261.

Shalizi, C. (2009). *Distances between clustering, hierarchical clustering* [Lecture notes]. https://www.stat.cmu.edu/~cshalizi/350/lectures/08/lecture-08.pdf

Soller, B. (2014). Caught in a bad romance: Adolescent romantic relationships and mental health. *Journal of Health and Social Behavior, 55*(1), 56–72. doi: 10.1177/0022146513520432

Stovel, K. (2001). Local sequential patterns: The structure of lynching in the deep South, 1882–1930. *Social Forces, 79*(3), 843–880. http://sf.oxfordjournals.org/content/79/3/843.short

Stovel, K., & Bolan, M. (2004). Residential trajectories using optimal alignment to reveal the structure of residential mobility. *Sociological Methods & Research, 32*(4), 559–598. doi: 10.1177/0049124103262683

Stovel, K., Savage, M., & Bearman, P. (1996). Ascription into achievement: Models of career systems at Lloyds Bank, 1890–1970. *American Journal of Sociology, 102*(2), 358–399. http://www.jstor.org/stable/10.2307/2782629

Struffolino, E. (2019). Navigating the early career: The social stratification of young workers' employment trajectories in Italy. *Research in Social Stratification and Mobility, 63.* doi: 10.1016/j.rssm.2019.100421

Struffolino, E., Bernardi, L., & Larenza, O. (2020). Lone parenthood and employment trajectories: A longitudinal mixed-method study. *Comparative Population Studies, 45,* 265–298.

Struffolino, E., Studer, M., & Fasang, A. E. (2016). Gender, education, and family life courses in East and West Germany: Insights from new sequence analysis techniques. *Advances in Life Course Research, 29,* 66–79.

Studer, M. (2013). WeightedCluster library manual: A practical guide to creating typologies of trajectories in the social sciences with R. *LIVES Working Papers, 24.* doi: 10.12682/lives.2296-1658.2013.24

Studer, M. (2015). Comment: On the use of globally interdependent multiple sequence analysis. *Sociological Methodology, 45*(1), 81–88. doi: 10.1177/0081175015588095

Studer, M. (2018). Divisive property-based and fuzzy clustering for sequence analysis. In G. Ritschard & M. Studer (Eds.), *Sequence analysis and related approaches: Innovative methods and applications* (pp. 223–239). Springer.

Studer, M. (2021). Validating sequence analysis typologies using parametric bootstrap. *Sociological Methodology, 51*(2), 290–318. doi: 10.1177/00811750211014232

Studer, M., Liefbroer, A. C., & Mooyaart, J. E. (2018). Understanding trends in family formation trajectories: An application of competing trajectories analysis (CTA). *Advances in Life Course Research, 36,* 1–12. doi: 10.1016/j.alcr .2018.02.003

Studer, M., & Ritschard, G. (2014). A comparative review of sequence dissimilarity measures. *LIVES Working Papers, 33.* doi: 10.12682/lives.2296-1658.2014.33

Studer, M., & Ritschard, G. (2016). What matters in differences between life trajectories: A comparative review of sequence dissimilarity measures. *Journal of the Royal Statistical Society: Series A (Statistics in Society), 179*(2), 481–511. http://onlinelibrary.wiley.com/doi/10.1111/rssa.12125/full

Studer, M., Ritschard, G., Gabadinho, A., & Müller, N. S. (2011). Discrepancy analysis of state sequences. *Sociological Methods & Research, 40*(3), 471–510. doi: 10.1177/0049124111415372

166

Studer, M., Struffolino, E., & Fasang, A. E. (2018). Estimating the relationship between time-varying covariates and trajectories: The sequence analysis multistate model procedure. *Sociological Methodology, 48*(1), 103–135. doi: 10.1177/0081175017747122

Tufte, E. R. (1983). *The visual display of quantitative information*. Graphics Press.

Van Winkle, Z. (2018). Family trajectories across time and space: Increasing complexity in family life courses in Europe? *Demography, 55*(1), 135–164. doi: 10.1007/s13524-017-0628-5

Van Winkle, Z., & Fasang, A. E. (2017). Complexity in employment life courses in Europe in the twentieth century—Large cross-national differences but little change across birth cohorts. *Social Forces, 96*(1), 1–30. doi: 10.1093/sf/sox032

Vanhoutte, B., Wahrendorf, M., & Prattley, J. (2018). Sequence analysis of life history data. In P. Liamputtong (Ed.), *Handbook of research methods in health social sciences* (pp. 1–19). Springer Singapore. doi: 10.1007/978-981-10-2779-6_146-1

Vrotsou, K., Ynnerman, A., & Cooper, M. (2014). Are we what we do? Exploring group behaviour through user-defined event-sequence similarity. *Information Visualization, 13*(3), 232–247.

Ward, J. H. (1963). Hierarchical grouping to optimize an objective function. *Journal of the American Statistical Association, 58*(301), 236–244.

Warren, J. R., Liying, L., Halpern-Manners, A., Raymo, J. M., & Palloni, A. (2015). Do different methods for modeling age-graded trajectories yield consistent and valid results? *American Journal of Sociology, 120*(6), 1809–1856.

Wickham, H. (2016). *ggplot2: Elegant graphics for data analysis*. Springer.

Wilson, M. C. (2014). Governance built step-by-step: Analysing sequences to explain democratization. In P. Blanchard, F. Bühlmann, & J.-A. Gauthier (Eds.), *Advances in sequence analysis: Theory, method, applications* (pp. 213–227). Springer International. doi: 10.1007/978-3-319-04969-4_11

Wu, L. L. (2000). Some comments on "Sequence analysis and optimal matching methods in sociology: Review and prospect." *Sociological Methods & Research, 29*(1), 41–64. doi: 10.1177/0049124100029001003

Zeileis, A., Fisher, J. C., Hornik, K., Ihaka, R., McWhite, C. D., Murrell, P., Stauffer, R., & Wilke, C. O. (2019). *colorspace: A toolbox for manipulating and assessing colors and palettes.* http://arxiv.org/abs/1903.06490

Zeileis, A., Hornik, K., & Murrell, P. (2009). Escaping RGBland: Selecting colors for statistical graphics. *Computational Statistics & Data Analysis, 53*(9), 3259–3270. doi: 10.1016/j.csda.2008.11.033

INDEX